Dash Diet Slow Cooker Cookbook

Simple No-Fuss Delicious Slow Cooker Recipes Made By Your Crock Pot To Rapid Weight Loss and Upgrade Your Lifestyle

By Peter Moore

Table of Contents

DELICIOUS POULTRY & SEAFOOD...50

BEEF AND PORK...64

Introduction

Thank you and congratulate you for choosing this Complete guide of Dash Diet Slow Cooker Cookbook! Hope it will help you a lot in your lifetime!

At first, please allow me to ask you some questions:
Do you have overweight for a long time? Have you ever tried any other diets to lose weight? **Do you feel tired sometime?**
Do you have acne or other skin disease?
Do you have high blood pressure?
Do you have no time to cook foods?
Are you busy working everyday?
Do you want to have delicious and nutritious foods when back home?

If the answer is yes for any of above questions, then this book is for you!

DASH Diet meas Dietary Approaches to Stop Hypertension. The DASH Diet is an approach to eating in a way that helps regulate hypertension. It is the conscious choice to eat healthy food in order to prevent pre-hypertension and control hypertension itself. Primarily, the DASH diet focuses on reducing the intake of sodium, which helps lower blood pressure.

By following such a diet plan, we can also avoid heart and kidney diseases, amongst a variety of other benefits. So what will you know about Dash Diet in this book?

1. The Definition Of Dash Diet
2. Benefits Of Dash Diet
3. The History And Current Craze Of Dash Diet
4. Why Dash Diet Promotes Weight Loss
5. Tips For Successful Dash Diet Journey
6. Foods Allowed/ Avoid
7. More And More...

We have helped thousands of people lose their weight, lower their blood pressure and have a healthy body by this amazing book! It will be your good companion!

As this book is mainly related to DASH Diet Slow Cooker. You will know much knowledge of slow cooker. If you often have no enough time to cook, then you may need a Slow cooker, which is a popular cooking appliance nowadays. Why so popular now? As it has too many benefits when using a slow cooker. You will know the benefits when reading this book. So what will you know about slow cooker in this book?

1. What Is a Slow Cooker
2. The Popularity Of The Slow Cooker
3. How To Choose a Good Slow Cooker
4. How To Use a Slow Cooker Properly
5. Maintenance Of a Slow Cooker
6. Benefits Of a Slow Cooker
7. Dos & Don'ts When Using Slow Cooker
8. Where To Buy a Proper Slow Cooker
9. More And More

We have written all of what we have known about Dash Diet and Slow Cooker. You will know the amazing result in next few days if you put this book into action!

Finally, you will find **100** Dash Diet Slow Cooker recipes which will support your Dash Diet journey! All the recipes are easy to make, they are delicious, nutritional, and good for your health! All the ingredients are easy to find in your local market. You can make your favorite dishes as per the step by step procedure. Or you can change the ingredients of the recipe when you are an experienced cooker. You know how to cook foods that you are really like!

For more detailed and useful information, please read the rest of this book! Welcome to the Dash Diet world!

DASH Diet

Basics of the DASH Diet

The DASH Diet is an approach to eating in a way that helps regulate hypertension. It is the conscious choice to eat healthy food in order to prevent pre-hypertension and control hypertension itself. Primarily, the DASH diet focuses on reducing the intake of sodium, which helps lower blood pressure.

DASH is a well-balanced dietary approach that most of people can follow. It also focuses upon the regular intake of nutrients such as magnesium, calcium and potassium which offer an array of benefits to all who follows the plan.

Of all the 38 healthy diet plans nowadays, the DASH diet has been recognized as the best diet plan for a healthy living lifestyle. It is also recommended for controlling diabetes and contributing to good heart health.

The DASH diet primarily focuses on the intake of plants, fruits, vegetables, whole grains and low fat dairy products. It helps you decide your weekly, monthly and thus yearly nutritional goals and how to achieve the results.

It can be adopted by both vegetarians and non-vegetarians and offers flexibility to meet meal preferences.

Definition Of The DASH Diet

DASH: Dietary Approaches to Stop Hypertension

As the famous saying goes, "a journey of a thousand miles begins with a single step." When an individual makes up his mind to live a healthy lifestyle, he needs to ensure that he accepts, ensures and chooses to be on a nutrition-rich, balanced and healthy diet.

DASH dieting is simply taking care to identify food-based strategies to reduce blood pressure.

It contains a sequence of instructions that an individual has to follow to enjoy all the benefits that this diet plan proposes. To ensure that one attains the goals set for oneself, several factors must be considered, such as:

- Hard work in terms of sticking to the diet plan is required to achieve favorable results
- Self discipline must be exercised to ensure the timely intake of meals
- It helps to use reminders as well as alarms to keep tabs on progress
- Daily instructions must be religiously followed, depending on individual the eating plans

The DASH diet emphasizes the consumption of fruits (to increase fiber intake and produce sufficient energy), whole grains (excellent sources of fiber and nutrients), dairy products (sources of Vitamin D, calcium and protein), vegetables (for magnesium, fiber, vitamins and potassium), nuts and seeds (contain saturated fat, protein, phytochemicals), and fish and meat (for zinc, iron, protein).

The DASH diet can be as effective as medications when it comes to regulation of blood pressure and cholesterol. The lower the intake of sodium, the lower the blood pressure.

The DASH diet also restricts consumption of fat (meats, dairy), sugar, sugar-based beverages, sweets and salt.

Although the DASH diet is not as effective as low carbohydrates diets in terms of losing weight, if an individual follows this diet plan to the T and adds an exercise routine, he can lose weight and improve both metabolism and sensitivity to insulin.

The History And Current Popularity Of The DASH Diet

According to medical studies and research, approximately 50 million people in the United States and close to 1 billion people worldwide are affected by hypertension.

There is a close relationship between blood pressure and the risk of cardio vascular disease. The higher and more unregulated the blood pressure, the greater the chances of heart failure, heart attack, strokes and kidney diseases.

Taking such medical conditions into consideration, the National Institutes of Health (United States) in 1992 began collaborating with five of the best medical research associations across the states to study and identify a method for controlling blood pressure.

Several different diet plans were studied, compared and experimented with. The team, after much research and many studies, concluded that diet plans with a high intake of fiber and certain minerals can drastically reduce blood pressure. This is how the DASH diet came into being.

The DASH diet also includes in its meal plans certain food choices that are high in anti-oxidants that can help prevent health problems such as cancer. It became extremely popular due to a number of benefits such as weight loss, prevention of cancer, a reduction in effects of diabetes, lowering LDL cholesterol, and prevention of cardio-vascular diseases as well as the formation of kidney stones.

It was well accepted by the general public as a highly successful dietary plan. Staying on the DASH diet and eating healthy foods can make you look younger than your age and keep diseases at bay. How you treat your body can determine how old your body looks; healthy eating habits can reverse the premature symptoms and consequences of ageing.

Advantages Of The DASH Diet

The DASH diet provides a healthy way of eating that has made it one of the most successful diet plans across the globe. It offers several health benefits, listed below:

- As it focuses on the reduction of sodium intake, it assists in a drastic reduction in blood pressure
- If accompanied by a regular exercise routine, it can facilitate weight loss and improvement in metabolism, However, one must make sure that the calorie consumption is low enough to aids the process
- Food choices that are rich in antioxidants aid in the prevention of serious medical conditions like cancer
- Controlled food choices and intake assist in reducing the effects of diabetes
- Since the diet plan emphasizes the low consumption of sodium along with consuming unsaturated and healthy fats, it helps get rid of LDL cholesterol
- One of the major benefits that the DASH diet offers is prevention of cardio vascular diseases, heart attacks, heart failure, and strokes
- It aids in improving the health of kidneys and prevents the formation of kidney stones
- Food choices rich in nutrients such as magnesium, potassium, calcium, protein, vitamins and certain phytochemicals promote a healthy mind along with a healthy body
- The diet can be followed by everyone in the family as the diet meals are easy. People of all ages can diet without any ill effects.

Why The DASH Diet Promotes
Fast Weight Loss

In addition to all its other health benefits, the DASH diet supports healthy weight loss. This is one of the major reasons for its popularity. Although the DASH diet wasn't formulated primarily for weight loss, such as the Atkins and Paleo diets, among others, if accompanied by an exercise routine, it can facilitate quick and healthy weight loss.

The advantage of the DASH diet is that it helps in weight loss and simultaneously aims towards overall healthiness. It encompasses a systematic approach towards food intake, focusing on certain food choices that aid weight loss while avoiding foods that lead to weight gain. It can also help wean oneself off blood pressure and diabetes medications.

The DASH diet includes lots of vegetables and fruits in its meal plans. Fruits and vegetables are typically low in calories, high in fiber, and are satiating. A weight loss drink or supplement can help you lose weight; however, it will not satiate your hunger. Therefore you are likely to eat more frequently, so your calorie intake will go up.

The diet includes certain protein rich-foods at each meal orsnack that are likewise filling, avoiding either in-between meals or blood sugar crashes due to a sudden spike of insulin.

The meal plans of the DASH diet are not overloaded with carbohydrates. The plans are generally low on starchy foods, instead including protein rich-foods that prevent muscle breakdown and boost the metabolism for faster weight loss.

Should you need more information than is contained here, there is a plethora of books, articles and journals available online that can provide additional plans and menus. If followed rigorously, they can help you achieve your desired results.

Important Tips For A Successful DASH Diet

Let us talk about some tips and strategies that help you get started on your voyage to successfully follow DASH diet plans. These tips will allow you to stay on track, monitor your progress and help you keep focused. The idea is that you shouldn't feel that you are on a certain diet plan. They do make sense and are simple to follow.

- **Make gradual changes**: Small and slight changes here and there should be adopted initially as you become accustomed to DASH diet. You can start by switching to consume 1-2 servings of fruits and vegetables so the body adapts to the change. You can cut down on meat intake slowly by half or a third and then later progress further
- **Reward successes**: Perfection takes time. Since the DASH diet will be new to you, expect certain road blocks which may result in slipups. You should try to understand what caused the setbacks. Be easy on yourself! Frequently reward yourself with a non-food treat for small accomplishments
- **Add an exercise routine**: The DASH diet should be combined with physical activities that will assist in lowering blood pressure, increasing metabolism and boosting immunity. Prepare a routine and include physical exercises that will keep you in good shape, burn unwanted calories and hence prevent obesity
- **Seek Support**: Seek assistance from doctors, friends or physicians if you are having a hard time sticking to the diet plan. Counseling and support sessions will boost your morale and confidence, and will provide room for improving further
- **Track calories and nutrition:** Practice the habit of going through nutrition labels so you are aware of sodium intake. One should aim for food and meals with less than 5% of recommended sodium daily value.

Compared to Paleo, Atkins and other famous diet plans, DASH doesn't involve partial or complete restrictions of certain foods. A dieter should gradually increase the intake of fruits, veggies and dairy (low fat), along with consumption of seeds, nuts, poultry, whole grains and fish, ensuring that sodium intake doesn't go beyond 2200-2300 milligrams perday. Try to refrain from high fat food, red meat and sugary carbonated drinks.

DASH requires the dieter to consume certain numbers and amount of servings chosen from different food groups. Again, the number of servings, which is primarily calorie intake, should be based on individual goals, such as a healthy lifestyle, getting rid of medical conditions or weight loss.

Foods Allowed On The DASH Diet

The following foods should be consumed daily to receive all benefits of the DASH diet.

Vegetables: 4-5 servings of fresh vegetables such as tomatoes, broccoli, carrots, sweet potatoes and leafy vegetables should be consumed as they are high in vitamin, magnesium, potassium and fibers. In the case of canned vegetables, check the nutritional label and avoid products with added salt.

Fruits: A minimum of 4-5 servings of fruits is recommended to provide necessary fibers and the required energy for the body to carry out daily functions. Fruits could be fresh, dried, frozen or canned. In the case of canned fruits or juices, carefully go through the nutritional label to avoid added sugars. For high quotients of fiber and anti-oxidants try including fruits such as apples, grapefruit and pears. Also try including fruits with low sugar levels. Most fruits have good quantities of magnesium, fiber and potassium and are low in fat.

Dairy: Dairy products such as milk, yogurt and cheese contain protein, calcium, Vitamin D and fat. Aim at a daily serving of 2-3 of low fat or fat free dairy. Dieter may also choose lactose free dairy in case he is intolerant to lactose and have troubles with dairy digestion.

Whole Grains: Recommended consumption of grains is 7-8 servings/day. Whole grains provide more nutrients and fiber than more processed products, so aim at 100% whole-wheat/grain. You can choose from a variety of cereals, pasta and bread; however, avoid topping them with cheese, cream or butter.

Nuts and Seeds: 5-6 servings per week of beans, legumes, seeds and nuts is recommended. They are good sources of phytochemicals, potassium, magnesium, protein and fiber. These nutrients help fight and prevent heart diseases and cancer. Foods in this category especially rich in these nutrients are cashews, almonds, peas, pistachios, peanuts, lentils and kidney beans. As they are also high on calories, one must consume them in small quantities.

Oils and Fats: A minimum of 2-3 servings per day is recommended in the DASH diet. The human body needs fats to absorb nutrients and they also strengthen the immune system. However, the intake should be controlled and limited as they also can lead to cardiovascular disease, diabetes and obesity. One must also be aware of the difference between saturated fat and transfats for better health.

Lean meat, fish and poultry: Up to 6 servings per day of fish, poultry and lean meat is advised. Lean and skinless meat is a source of protein, zinc, iron and B complex vitamins. Fish such as salmon, tuna and herring are recommended as they are rich in Omega 3 fatty acids that can lower cholesterol levels in blood. Try eating them roasted, baked or grilled, but avoid fried.

Alcohol: Recommended for men is not more than two drinks and for women is one drink or less per day. Also limit intake of caffeine as it inflates the blood pressure temporarily.

Sweets: A maximum of 5 servings (or even less if possible) per week is advised. The DASH diet does not require abstaining from sweets totally. However, dieters should keep a check on sweets intake and choose those with lesser fat, such as fruit ices, jelly beans, low-fat cookies and granola bars. Use of artificial sweetener should be curbed, gradually reduced if necessary.

Foods To Avoid On The DASH Diet

In choosing a healthy lifestyle to gain all the benefits the DASH diet offers, a few food items should be avoided. Rejecting foods which have adverse effects should only make sense. Below is a list of such food items:

- Sugary beverages

- Artificial sweeteners
- Salted nuts or seeds
- High fat snacks
- Dairy with high fat, or whole cream or milk
- High sodium salad dressings
- In addition, the following should be reduced or eliminated: Red meat
- Caffeine
- Smoking

DIET (LISTED AND EXPLAINED)

FOOD GROUP	DAILY SERVINGS	SERVING SIZES	EXAMPLES	SIGNIFICANCE
Grains	7 to 8	A slice of whole wheat bread	Whole wheat or brown bread	Source of fiber and energy
Vegetables	4 to 5	A cup of leafy vegetable 1/2 cup of cooked veggie 170 ml/6 oz of vegetable juice	Carrots Sweet Potatoes Tomatoes Broccoli Artichokes Kale	Source of fiber, potassium & magnesium
Fruits	4 to 5	Medium sized fruit 1/4 dried fruits 1/2 cup frozen/canned fruit 1/2 cup fruit juice	Apples Bananas Oranges Grapefruit Peaches Pears	Source of fiber, potassium & magnesium
Dairy (Low Fat/Fat Free)	2 to 3	A cup fat free milk A cup fat free yogurt 1/2 cup cheese	Skim Milk Skim Buttermilk Low Fat Yogurt Skim Mozzarella Cheese Nonfat Cheese	Source of protein and calcium
Fish, Meat & Poultry	Up to 6	1 1/2ounce cooked meat, fish or poultry 1 whole egg	Lean Meat (fat trimmed) Broiled, baked or	Source of magnesium and protein

		2 egg whites	roasted meat Skinless poultry Maximum 4 egg yolks per week	
Nuts & Seeds	5 to 6	1/3 cup nuts (without salt) 2 Tbsp nut butter 2 Tbsp seeds 1/2 cup legumes (cooked)	Almonds Cashews Pistachios Kidney Bean Sunflower Seeds Lentils	Source of energy, potassium, magnesium, fiber and protein
Fats & Oil	2 to 3	1 tsp margarine 2 Tbsp salad dressing 1 tsp mayonnaise 1 tsp vegetable oil	Margarine Low fat mayonnaise Light salad dressing Vegetable Oil	Omega 3 fatty acids, saturated fat
Sweets	Up to 5/week	1 Tbsp Sugar 1 Tbsp Jelly/Jam 1/2 oz jelly beans 1 cup lemon juice	Fruit Ice Jelly Bean Low Fat Cookies Granola Bars	Should be low on fat

FAQs

I am lactose intolerant. Can I follow the DASH diet?
Most lactose intolerant people tolerate cheese, yogurt and heated milk products and can also tolerate non-fat dairy. Lactose-free milk or milk substitutes such as soy or rice can also be used. Goat milk can be substituted for cow's milk for some people.
These substitutes should contain the same amount of Vitamin D and calcium as regular milk.

I am gluten intolerant. Can I follow the DASH diet?
Gluten-free products can be substituted for foods based on wheat. The DASH encourages unprocessed foods.

Does the DASH diet mean low fat and high fiber?

That is absolutely correct. The DASH diet encourages the consumption of more fiber and moderately low fat (unsaturated fats and Omega 3 fat products).

Can I have a vegan/vegetarian version of the DASH diet?

Nuts, seeds, legumes and beans can be substituted for poultry, meat and fish.

Do I need to follow a meal/recipe book while I am on the DASH diet? Can I replace or substitute meal choices?

Yes, meal choices can be substituted., However, keep in mind that the nutrients of the substitute should match the original in terms of minerals, vitamins, zinc, iron, magnesium, potassium, phytochemicals, etc.

Can I completely give up artificial sweeteners while on the DASH diet?

Yes, in fact, doing so will provide additional benefits. You can substitute sweeteners with such foods as melon chunks or sliced citrus fruits.

Can I substitute sea salt over regular sodium salt?

Often sea salt weighs more than regular salt, though it contains less sodium. It is best to improvise on seasoning food without added salt.

Can potassium-chloride-containing salts be used while on the DASH diet?

Only after consulting a physician as they are known to lead to excess potassium in the body.

Can potassium, magnesium and calcium supplements be used instead of DASH dieting?

Studies have shown that supplementing is less beneficial than DASH dieting. Also they have fewer or no effects on reducing cholesterol and heart disease.

Why A Slow Cooker?

What Is A Slow Cooker?

The slow cooker, commonly known as a crock pot, is one of the many widely used kitchen appliances used to cook meals by plugging the device to an electrical output, unlike the traditional methods of cooking on gas or electric stoves.

The technique most frequently used to cook food in a slow cooker involves preparation of the meal in hot liquid, usually for long hours.

Food is prepared at comparatively low temperature, so cooking takes many more hours than usual, when compared to boiling, frying or baking the food.

A slow cooker or crock pot is usually manufactured in either an oval or round shape and is typically made with a removable ceramic or porcelain interior. A metal exterior body contains the electrical element that produces heat. A glass lid covers the food during preparation.

Slow cookers come in different varieties and capacities, ranging from 500 ML to as much as 7 liters.

Most offer options for different heat settings such as low, medium, high; a few devices also have a "keep warm" setting.

The Popularity Of The Slow Cooker

The slow cooker was first developed by an American, Irving Naxon, who got the inspiration from his grandmother.

This idea was further developed by the Radiant Heat Corporation from New Jersey, which bought the concept and reintroduced the device with a new name, the crock pot.

The device gained a lot of popularity in the 1970s when many women began to focus on more on careers than homemaking.

For them the slow cooker speeded meal preparation so they could focus more on other priorities.

The slow cooker or crockpot doesn't require the cook to be around while the meal is prepared. As a result, it is a great choice for working women who would not want to spend time in preparation of food after spending long hours at work and taking care of other family and personal activities.

The best part is that the slow cooker can be used to prepare a variety of food and dishes and requires little or no expertise for that.

How To Choose A Good Slow Cooker

Here are a few pointers to be taken into consideration while choosing a cooker:-

- Slow cookers come in numerous sizes and varieties with different prices and advanced functions. To choose the right crock pot essentially depends on your personal requirements and how you wish to use the device in your daily life.
- It is best to avoid choosing crock pots that have the heating element on the bottom of the device. This prevents the even distribution of heat; it also requires the user to stir the dish frequently, eliminating the slow cooker's major advantage – being able to walk away and forget it. Better cookers have heating elements placed on the sides of the cooker.
- They come in numerous distinct materials such as metal, porcelain or ceramic. It is advisable to buy the cookers in which the crock is not attached to the heating element, which will ease the cleaning process of the unit.

- Glass lids allow you to have a clear vision of the dish without opening the lid. Frequent opening of the lid increases the t cooking time..
- Choosing a shape is a personal preference. Cooking meat is simpler in oval shaped cookers; round ones- are a perfect choice for vegetarian cooking.
- Choosing the size of the pot totally depends upon the quantity of food that you normally prepare which in turn depends upon the size of the family. A 6-8 quart size is suggested to be the best fit for household usage, keeping in mind that the cooker shouldn't be more than 50% full in order to get the best results while cooking.
- A cooker with either a digital timer or one that allows the user to pre set the time for cooking saves the user from having to be physically around while the dish is cooking. Also, advanced cookers switch off automatically once the preset time is reached, which ensures that the meal isn't burnt.

A few advanced cookers have a function known as 'keep warm'. As its name suggests, it keeps the meal warm once the pre-set time is achieved.

HOW TO USE A SLOW COOKER PROPERLY

Here are a few quick tips that will provide the user with a better experience:

- Since the primary benefit of the slow cooker is how easy it is to use, preparation beforehand will make it even easier: sautéing vegetables such as onions, leeks, and carrots, and browning meat before placing them in the cooker., However, this step is not always necessary and can be used as you desire.
- In cases where you are short of time, complete the preparation the night before and refrigerate overnight. Next morning, take out the food and leave it for about 15-20 minutes to approach room temperature. Then start the cooking process.
- Slow cookers are great for saving money by cooking cheaper cuts of pork, lamb, beef or chicken. Even if less meat is used, slow cooking spreads the meaty flavor through the entire dish. As a result, you can use more vegetables than meat.

- Adding oil or having fat on the meat isn't required in a slow cooker, or else you'll find oil in the dish. It is advised to trim the fat prior to the cooking. This would also result in a healthier product.
- Slow cookers require a lot less water than conventional cookers as the liquid cannot evaporate. Having the cooker filled up half or two-thirds at the maximum is good enough.
- It is also preferable to use the low heat settings more often than other settings as slower, longer cooking really brings out the best flavor of the ingredients and keeps the natural juices intact. This also means that the dish will take longer, but itwill still be cooked once you're back from work.
- For most recipes, you will put all ingredients in at one time at the beginning. However, rice, certain herbs, pasta, and similar ingredients might have to be added towards the latter half of the process.
- Root vegetables usually take longer than meat or other vegetables to cook, so they should be placed at the bottom of the cooker.

Maintenance Of A Slow Cooker

A slow cooker doesn't require a lot of cleaning, saving the user from the hassles of cleaning many utensils. All it requires is a cleanup every now and then, which isn't rigorous at all.

Because different crock pots are made up of different materials and require different cleaning treatments, read the manual that came with your cooker before cleaning it. Usually commonly available pantry items such as dish soap, baking soda, ammonia, white vinegar are all that it takes for the cleanup process.

Other equipment required to ease the process are a piece of cloth (preferably cotton or micro fiber), a scrub brush and a screw driver. Be sure to unplug the pot from the power socket before the clean up begins!

The exterior of the pot can be gently with a damp piece of cotton or micro fiber cloth. Avoid harsh treatment as it might damage the finish and the parts that put it together. Knobs, handles, lids, and other external fittings should be detached from the pot, using the screwdriver if necessary, and gently cleaned with soapy water and cloth.

Use baking soda in the case of stubborn stains on the exterior of the cooker. Clean the bottom of the cooker with scrub brush to eliminate any crumbs.

Fill the cooker with water and cook for an hour or two so any stubborn cooked on food will come off easily. The heating element should never be treated or dipped in water, but rather should be carefully cleaned with a damp cloth.

For stubborn or tough stains, add water with ammonia to the cooker and leave it covered overnight.

Benefits Of A Slow Cooker

A slow cooker offers a variety of advantages, although users must be aware that like the conventional way of cooking food, preparation may be required to be done in advance, often the previous night.

Meats should be browned on a stove, vegetables and/or fruits are to be washed, cleaned, diced, minced, chopped or treated as required.

Of all the advantages, the most significant is that once you place the ingredients in the cooker, you are only required to configure the heat settings and timer. Then you can forget about the whole thing, often for many hours till the food is cooked and ready to be served.

Also in advanced devices, once the food is cooked the device by itself changes the mode to 'keep warm' to ensure the food isn't overcooked and is ready to be served once it is out of the cooker. After work or recreational activites, you are welcomed home to a pre-cooked meal; all you have to do is serve and eat.

Since the ingredients (vegetables, meat, seasoning) are cooked for many hours on either low or medium heat settings, the food's natural flavor juices and nutrition are retained, contributing to a healthy mind and body.

Another benefit is that the usage of this device isn't restricted to any particular season or any specific time of the year. Rather, crock pots can be utilized throughout the year. In summers, it helps reduces the additional heat from the use of ovens and stoves.

It uses and emits less energy than conventional modes and devices for cooking food. After preparing the food, you wouldn't have to worry about cleaning lots of additional pots or utensils. As slow cooker or a crock pot is a single pot, so it helps reduce the use of water.

It offers a variety of dishes and meals to be cooked such as soups, stews, and casseroles. Using a slow cooker is very simple. As instructed above, the user prepares the veggies, meat, sauces, herbs, and seasoning, adds a liquid such as broth, wine and/or water (usually filling the pot one-third or one-half full) and puts it all in the cooker. Adjust the heat settings and timing and cover the cooker with the glass lid.

Some cookers have advanced settings to lower the heat if the set cooking time raises the internal temperature of the device beyond a specific point. Basic cookers require the user to change the heat and temperature modes manually, however, the advanced ones does it automatically.

Covering the pot guarantees that the vapor produced doesn't evaporate. Hence the vitamins, minerals and other essential nutrients which are water soluble don't leave the food. The also assists with the transfer of heat from the pot walls to the ingredients, giving a natural and distinct flavor to the dish.

Generally low temperature settings results in more tender and mouth-watering dishes. The real luxury for users is to configure the settings and forget all about it for hours till the dish is ready to be served and eaten.

Dos & Don'ts When Using Slow Cooker

Dos:
- Go through the recipe that you wish to cook so you have an idea how long the food needs to cook

- Wear oven mitts, as the cooker as well as lid tend to get very hot after long cooking hours
- Tender and delicate ingredients such as mushrooms, fish, peas, and similar items should be added to the cooker in the last hour so that they spread the flavor without getting too pulpy
- When the timer indicates that the cooking hours have finished, be sure to turn off the device before removing the meal from the cooker
- Spray the interior of the cooker with a non-stick spray to ease cleaning
- Foods that take longer to cook should be placed at the bottom. Water/broth/wine should be the last ingredient added to the cooker after all others
- Frozen foods should be thawed overnight before placing them to the cooker

Don'ts:
- Avoid stirring the food unless the recipe suggests doing so. One of the benefits that a slow cooker offers is that it keeps the dishes from sticking to the device without stirring
- Unless the recipe suggests, preheating the cooker isn't required
- Avoid leaving leftover food in the pot
- Avoid adding dairy products to the device until the last half hour as they have a tendency to separate and curdle
- Slow cookers shouldn't be more than half or two-thirds full as more filling can be dangerous
- Avoid putting cooker inserts on gas or electric stoves, or in a freezer
- Do not remove the lid while preparing the food until the required time for preparation is over

Where to Buy A Proper Slow Cooker

Users can order a device online. However, new users should be sure they know how to choose a good slow cooker by referring the pointers above.

Consulting sales people in department or hardware stores can help in the decision before making a purchase that matches your personal preferences.

DASH-Friendly Bread & Pasta

1. Chicken and Cheese Pasta

Cooking Time: 10 hrs.
Servings: 4-6

Nutrition Facts (Estimated Amount Per Serving)

315.4 Calories	487.9 mg Sodium	15.5 g Protein
6.4 g Total Fat	52.7 Carbohydrates	
20.1 Cholesterol	7.1 g Dietary Fiber	

INGREDIENTS
- 1 lb. Chicken Breast (skinless and boneless)
- 1 can Cream of Mushroom Soup
- 1 can Campbell's Cheddar Cheese Soup
- 1 box Rotini Pasta
- 1 cup Kraft blend of 2% Mexican cheese
- ½ cup fat-free Milk

DIRECTIONS:
- Place chicken breast in the slow cooker.
- Add seasonings.
- In a bowl, mix milk with the soups.
- Pour the mixture over the chicken breasts.
- You can cook this on either low or high --6 hrs. on high and 10 hrs. on low.
- Shred the chicken breast with the help of fork.
- Cook pasta per the instructions.
- Shred the cheese as well.
- Mix all the cooked and uncooked ingredients together.
- Serve warm.

2. Easiest Pasta and Broccoli

Cooking Time: 4 hrs 20 mins
Servings: 4-6

Nutrition Facts (Estimated Amount Per Serving)

289 Calories	104 mg Sodium	346 mg Potassium
7 g Total fat	48 g Carbohydrates	12 g Protein
1 g Saturated fat	5 g Dietary Fiber	

INGREDIENTS

- 12 oz. pasta, uncooked
- 2 tbsp. olive oil, divided
- 5 smashed and chopped cloves garlic,
- ¼ c. Romano cheese or Parmesan, grated
- 6 ½ c. fresh broccoli florets, no stems
- Salt and fresh cracked pepper to taste

DIRECTIONS:

- Boil salted water and cook broccoli and pasta together as pasta. When pasta is prepared, reserve a cup of the pasta cooking water. Drain broccoli and pasta.
- Heat a pot on high heat. Add a tbsp. of oil. As soon as it is hot, add garlic. Cook garlic until golden. Reduce the temperature to low, add pasta and broccoli and combine well.
- Add remaining olive oil and grated cheese. Combine in such a way that no large pieces of broccoli appear. Add a half-cup of the reserved pasta water and blend well, adding extra if desired. Add pepper and salt to taste.

Mouth-watering Curries, Chilies& Appetizers

---

3. Salsa Chicken

Cooking Time: 8 hrs.
Servings: About 6

Nutrition Facts (Estimated Amount Per Serving)

281.5 Calories   907.2 mg Sodium   35.7 g Protein
7.3 g Total Fat   18.2 g Carbohydrates
139.4 mg Cholesterol   3.3 g Dietary Fiber

INGREDIENTS

- 2 lb. Chicken Thighs or Breasts (skin and boneless)
- 2 cups Salsa
- 15 ¼ oz. Corn
- 10 oz. each Green Chile and diced Tomatoes
- 1 chopped Onion (small)
- 1 tsp. Chili powder
- 1 tsp. Onion powder
- 1 tsp. Garlic powder
- ½ tsp. Red Pepper
- 1 tsp. dried Oregano
- 1 tsp. ground Cumin

DIRECTIONS

- Place Chicken in the cooker.
- Add the spices
- Add the chopped onion.
- Place rest of the ingredients in the slow cooker.
- Set the cooker on low heat and cook for 7 or 8 hrs.
- Serve hot

4. Hot Chicken

Cooking Time: 7 hrs 20 mins
Servings: About 4

Nutrition Facts (Estimated Amount Per Serving)
187.8 Calories
1.5 g Total Fat
65.7 mg Cholesterol
471.3 mg Sodium
15.3 mg Carbohydrates
0.7 g Dietary Fiber
26.6 g Protein

INGREDIENTS
- 1 lb Chicken Breast
- 1 chopped Onion (large)
- ½ cup Ketchup (low carb)
- 3 tbsp. Brown Sugar
- Diet Pepsi (1 can)
- Bread

DIRECTIONS
- Place all the ingredients in the slow cooker.
- Start cooking the chicken on "low" heat.
- Allow it to cook for 6 hrs.
- When the chicken is cooked, transfer it to plate and shred it well.
- Place the chicken in the cooker and cook again for 1 hr.
- Serve hot with bread.

5. Delicious Chicken

Cooking Time: 10 hrs
Servings: About 6

Nutrition Facts (Estimated Amount Per Serving)

234.2 Calories   466.4 mg Sodium   24.3 g Protein
8.1 g Total Fat   11 mg Carbohydrates
74.7 mg Cholesterol   0.8 g Dietary Fiber

INGREDIENTS

- 1 lb Chicken Breast (skinless and boneless)
- 10 ¾ oz. Cream of Chicken Soup
- 10 ¾ oz. Cream of Mushroom Soup
- ½ cup of White Wine
- 1 cup Sour Cream)
- ½ tsp. Celery Salt
- ½ tsp. Paprika
- 1 tsp. Salt
- 1 tsp. Garlic Powder
- Parmesan Cheese, grated
- Pepper to taste

DIRECTIONS

- Place chicken in cooker.
- Coat with seasoning.
- In a bowl, mix soups.
- Pour the soup mix over the chicken.
- Cook on "low" for 10 hrs.
- Transfer the chicken into the plate and stir sour cream into liquid in the cooker.
- Again, add the chicken into the cooker.
- Garnish with cheese while serving.
- Serve hot.

6. Chicken with Noodles

Cooking Time: 8 hrs 30 mins
Servings: About 8

Nutrition Facts (Estimated Amount Per Serving)
315.9 Calories   418.2 mg Sodium   27 g Protein
7.3 g Total Fat   37.3 mg Carbohydrates
94.9 mg Cholesterol   5.1 g Dietary Fiber

INGREDIENTS
- 6 boneless Chicken Legs
- Diced Carrots
- 10 oz Corn (frozen)
- 10 oz Peas (frozen)
- 1 tsp. Basil
- 1 chopped Onion (small)
- 1 can Cream of Chicken Soup
- 3 cups Noodles
- Water
- Salt

DIRECTIONS
- In a cooker, place carrots on the bottom.
- Put the chicken on top of the carrots.
- Add water to cover and cook on high for 8 hrs.
- Transfer the chicken to a plate.
- Drain the water.
- Place the chicken back into the cooker.
- Now, pour the chicken soup over the chicken along with water (2 cans).
- Add i basil, corn and onion. Add water to cover the vegetables.
- Cook for 8 hrs on low.
- Place noodles in the cooker.
- Cook again for 25 mins on "high".
- Serve hot.

7. Chili Con Carne

Cooking Time: 6 hrs
Servings: 6

Nutrition Facts (Estimated Amount Per Serving)

216.1 Calories	480.7 mg Sodium	18.8 g Protein
5.1 g Total Fat	21.8 mg Carbohydrates	
43.4 mg Cholesterol	2.5 g Dietary Fiber	

INGREDIENTS

For Spice Paste:
- 2 tbs. Chili Powder
- 1 tsp. Chipotle Powder
- 1 tbsp. Cumin
- 2 tsp. Cocoa Powder (unsweetened)
- 1 tsp. Cornmeal
- 1 chopped Jalapeño
- 3 tbsp. Water

For Chili:
- 1 tbsp. Vegetable Oil
- 12 ounces Beef Sirloin (cubed)
- 1 chopped Onion (large)
- 2 cloves Garlic
- 14.5 ounces Tomatoes (diced)
- 14.5 ounces Kidney Beans (Red)
- 14.5 ounces Northern Beans
- 2 diced Carrots
- 2 cups Chicken Stock (homemade recommended)

DIRECTIONS
- Blend spices and water into a paste in a food processor.
- Oil a sauté pan.

- Brown the beef in the pan.
- Transfer the beef into the slow cooker.
- Now, place onions the pan.
- Sauté for at least 5 mins.
- Pour the spice paste into the pan.
- Stir well.
- Transfer the paste mix to the slow cooker.
- Add the chicken stock.
- Put remaining ingredients in the cooker and cook for 6 hrs.
- Serve hot.

8. Pinto and Black Bean Chili

Cooking Time: 4 hrs 30 mins
Servings: 8

Nutrition Facts (Estimated Amount Per Serving)
217.3 Calories
4.7 g Total Fat
0 mg Cholesterol
269.1 mg Sodium
26.8 mg Carbohydrates
8.3 g Dietary Fiber
18.9 g Protein

INGREDIENTS
- 1 pound Ground Turkey
- 1 chopped Onion
- 1 minced clove Garlic
- 1 chopped Green Pepper
- 1 tsp. Oregano
- ½ tsp. Cumin
- 1 ½ tsp. Cayenne Pepper
- 1 tsp. Black Pepper
- 14.5 oz can rinsed Black Beans
- 14.5 oz can rinsed Pinto Beans
- 29 oz diced Tomatoes

DIRECTIONS
- Make balls of the ground Turkey. Place them in slow cooker.
- Add rest of the ingredients to the slow cooker.
- Add ¾ can water.
- Cook turkey on "high" for 4 hrs.
- Serve hot.

9. Chicken Stroganoff

Cooking Time: 7 hrs
Servings: 4-6

Nutrition Facts (Estimated Amount Per Serving)
217.3 Calories
4.7 g Total Fat
0 mg Cholesterol
269.1 mg Sodium
26.8 mg Carbohydrates
8.3 g Dietary Fiber
18.9 g Protein

INGREDIENTS
- 1 lb. Chicken Breasts (skinless and boneless)
- 1 can fat-free Mushroom Soup
- 16 oz. fat-free Sour Cream
- 1 package dry Onion Soup Mix

DIRECTIONS
- Arrange chicken on the bottom of the slow cooker.
- In a bowl, mix soups along with sour cream.
- Pour this mix over the Chicken.
- Cook on "low" for 7 hrs. Serve hot.

10. Chili Beans and Sweet Potato

Cooking Time: 6 hrs 30 mins
Servings: About 8

Nutrition Facts (Estimated Amount Per Serving)

330.1 Calories

4.9 g Total Fat

0 mg Cholesterol

873.2 mg Sodium

58.2 mg Carbohydrates

16.7 g Dietary Fiber

16.8 g Protein

INGREDIENTS

- 2 tbsp. Olive Oil
- 4 minced cloves Garlic
- 2 tsp. Sea Salt
- 1 cubed Sweet Potato (large)
- 3 chopped Carrots (small)
- 28 oz. Tomatoes, diced with juice
- 60 oz. canned, drained Black Beans
- 1 tbsp. Cumin
- 1 tbsp. Chili Powder
- 1 tsp. Cocoa Powder
- 1 cup Water

DIRECTIONS

- In a pan, sauté garlic and onion in oil. Add in the salt.
- Add remaining vegetables.
- Put the beans in the slow cooker.
- Put in the onion mixture as well.
- Cook on "high" for 6 hrs.
- Stir once and add 1 cup of Water.
- Cook again for 30 mins.
- Serve hot.

11. Spaghetti and Vegetable Sauce

CookingTime: 8 hrs
Servings: About 12
Nutrition Facts (Estimated Amount Per Serving)
30.8 Calories
4g Total Fat
0 mg Cholesterol
531.1 mg Sodium
7.5 mg Carbohydrates
1.7 g Dietary Fiber
1.6 g Protein

INGREDIENTS

- 1 cup Vegetable Protein
- 1 can Tomatoes (diced)
- 2 large cans Tomato Sauce
- 2 ¼ tsp. Salt
- ¼ tsp. Pepper
- 2 tsp. Sugar
- ¼ tsp. Oregano
- ¼ tsp. Chilies (crushed)
- ¼ tsp. Basil
- ¼ tsp. Garlic Powder
- 1 tbsp. Mustard (dry)
- ¼ cup chopped Onion
- ¼ cup chopped Green Pepper
- ¼ cup chopped Mushrooms

DIRECTIONS

- At first, soak the protein i 1 cup of water.
- Place all the ingredients in the slow cooker.
- Add in the protein.
- Cook n "low" for 8 hrs.
- Serve hot with spaghetti.

12. Slow Cooker Chicken Soup

Cooking Time: 4 hrs
Servings: About 5

Nutrition Facts (Estimated Amount Per Serving)
246 Calories
6 g Total Fat
32 mg Cholesterol
467 mg Sodium
29 mg Carbohydrates
5 g Dietary Fiber
11 g Protein

INGREDIENTS
- 1 diced Carrot
- 1 chopped Celery Stalk
- 1 sliced Onion
- 4 pounds Chicken Legs
- 6 Parsley Sprigs
- 2 Thyme Sprigs
- Bay Leaf
- 20 Peppercorns (whole)
- 1 crushed clove of Garlic
- 9 cups Water

DIRECTIONS
- Place all the ingredients in the slow cooker.
- Cook on "High" for 4 hrs.
- Serve hot.

13. Chicken Cacciatore

Cooking Time: 4 hrs 25 mins
Servings: About 6

Nutrition Facts (Estimated Amount Per Serving)
277 Calories
11 g Total Fat
85 mg Cholesterol
463 mg Sodium
15 mg Carbohydrates
2 g Dietary Fiber
29 g Protein

INGREDIENTS
- 1/3 cup of all-purpose Flour
- 1 broiler Chicken
- 2 tbsp. Canola Oil
- 2 sliced Onions
- 1 sliced Green Pepper
- 6 oz. Mushroom
- 14 oz. Tomatoes (diced)
- 2 minced cloves Garlic
- Salt
- ½ tsp. Oregano (dried)
- ¼ tsp. Basil (dried)
- ½ cup Parmesan cheese, shredded

DIRECTIONS
- Coat chicken with flour by tossing in a plastic bag.
- Now, brown the chicken in a skillet.
- Transfer it to the slow cooker.
- Place the rest of the ingredients over the chicken.
- Cook on "low" for 4 hrs.
- Serve hot after garnishing with Parmesan.

14. Fluffy Potatoes

Cooking Time: 4 hrs 20 mins
Servings: About 5

Nutrition Facts (Estimated Amount Per Serving)
278 Calories
10 g Total Fat
134 mg Cholesterol
270 mg Sodium
8 mg Carbohydrates
0 g Dietary Fiber
32 g Protein

INGREDIENTS
- 2 lbs. Red Potatoes
- Olive Oil
- Rosemary
- 2/3 cup Buttermilk
- ½ cup Yogurt (Greek)
- 1/8 tsp. Baking Powder

DIRECTIONS
- Peel the potatoes.
- Add olive oil and rosemary.
- Place them in slow cooker, covering with parchment paper.
- Cook on "low" for 4 hrs.
- When cooked, add yogurt along with the buttermilk and mash well.
- You can add baking powder in the mashed potatoes for a fluffier texture.
- Serve hot.

15. Yummy Chuck Roast

Cooking Time: 8 hrs 50 mins
Servings: 8-10

Nutrition Facts (Estimated Amount Per Serving)

220 Calories   189 mg Sodium   30 g Protein
16 g Total Fat   13 mg Carbohydrates
8 mg Cholesterol   3 g Dietary Fiber

INGREDIENTS

- 1 pound halved Mushrooms
- Black Pepper
- 2 pounds Chuck Roast
- 2 tbsp. Cornstarch
- 1 chopped Onion
- ½ cup low-fat Sour Cream
- 2 tbsp. Dijon Mustard
- 2 tbsp. Dill Weed, chopped

DIRECTIONS

- Sauté mushrooms, onion and beef along with the salt and pepper in a pan.
- Place in the slow cooker.
- Cook on "low" for 8 hrs. Stir when done.
- In a bowl, mix cornstarch with 2 cups of water.
- Boil starch mixture in a pan for 1 min.
- When beef is done, add starch mixture and rest of the ingredients to the slow cooker.
- Serve the beef on the heated plates after garnishing with dill

16. Paprika Goulash

Cooking Time: 5 hrs 30 mins
Servings: 8

Nutrition Facts (Estimated Amount Per Serving)

149 Calories	122 mg Sodium	21 g Protein
9 g Total Fat	6 mg Carbohydrates	
40 mg Cholesterol	2 g Dietary Fiber	

INGREDIENTS

- 4 tbsp. smoked Hungarian Paprika
- 2 tsp. dried Thyme
- 1 tsp. ground Black Pepper
- 1 ¼ pounds cubed Pork Loin
- 1 tbsp. Olive Oil
- 3 sliced Onions
- 3 chopped cloves Garlic
- ¾ cup Water
- ¾ cup Tomato Puree
- 1 cup of Greek-style Yogurt

DIRECTIONS

- Combine the seasoning in a bowl.
- Coat the pork cubes in the seasoning.
- Sauté garlic and onion in 1 tbsp. oil for 4 mins.
- Add the pork and cook for 6 mins.
- Transfer the pork mixture to the slow cooker.
- In same pan, pour puree along with the water.
- Pour the puree mixture to the slow cooker.
- Cook on "low" for 8 hrs.
- Serve with yogurt.

17. Saag

Cooking Time: 4 hrs
Servings: 8

Nutrition Facts (Estimated Amount Per Serving)

138 Calories	59 mg Sodium	3 g Protein
21 g Total Fat	8 mg Carbohydrates	
0 mg Cholesterol	1 g Dietary Fiber	

INGREDIENTS

- 3 tbsp. minced Ginger
- 1 tbsp. Garam Masala
- 4 minced cloves Garlic
- 1 ½ cup Tomato Puree
- 1 tbsp. Cumin (ground)
- 1 tbsp. Coriander (ground)
- ¼ tsp. Kosher Salt
- ¼ tsp. Cayenne Pepper
- 15 ounces Coconut Milk
- 20 ounces Baby Spinach
- 30 ounces cubed Tofu
- ½ cup thawed Peas
- Cilantro (chopped)

DIRECTIONS

- Except tofu, coriander and peas. Place all the ingredients except tofu, coriander and peas in the slow cooker and cook on "low" for 3 hrs.
- Add in the rest of the ingredients.
- Uncover the cooker and cook again on "low" for 1 hr.
- Garnish with cilantro.
- Serve hot.

18. Ratatouille

Cooking Time: 5 hrs 30 mins
Servings: About 4

Nutrition Facts (Estimated Amount Per Serving)

98 Calories	115 mg Sodium	8 g Protein
33 g Total Fat	14 mg Carbohydrates	
1 mg Cholesterol	3 g Dietary Fiber	

INGREDIENTS
- 2 tbsp. Olive Oil
- 2 cups Eggplant (cubed)
- 1 chopped Onion
- 4 minced cloves Garlic
- 2 tbsp. chopped Tarragon
- 2 tbsp. chopped Parsley
- 1 cubed Zucchini
- 1 sliced red Bell Pepper (red)
- ½ tsp. ground Black Pepper
- 14 ounce can diced Tomatoes

DIRECTIONS
- Sauté eggplant for 5 mins in 1 tbsp. of oil.
- Transfer the eggplant to the slow cooker.
- Now, sauté garlic and onion in rest of the oil for 6 mins.
- Transfer them to slow cooker as well.
- Add in the rest of the ingredients.
- Cook on "low" for 4.5 hrs.
- Serve warm.

19. Garlic and Broccoli Omelets

Cooking Time: 1 hr & 20 mins
Servings: About 2

Nutrition Facts (Estimated Amount Per Serving)

493 Calories   984 mg Sodium   29 g Protein
5 g Total Fats   6 mg Carbohydrates
205 mg Cholesterol   3 g Dietary Fiber

INGREDIENTS

- 4 Egg whites
- 2 Eggs
- 2 tbsp. Olive Oil
- 2 minced cloves Garlic
- ½ tsp. of Red Pepper Flakes
- ½ cup low-fat Feta Cheese
- Ground Black Pepper
- 1 cup chopped Broccoli

DIRECTIONS

- In a bowl, beat the egg whites and eggs.
- Sauté broccoli in oil for 2 mins. Add in the pepper flakes and garlic. You can add black pepper as well.
- Remove from heat.
- Pour the prepared egg white mixture in the slow cooker.
- Cook on "low" for 1 hr.
- Now, arrange the cooked broccoli mixture on the egg layer.
- Cover and cook again on "low" for 30 more mins.
- Serve immediately.

20. Bulgur Chili

Cooking Time: 4 hrs & 30 mins
Servings: 2

Nutrition Facts (Estimated Amount Per Serving)

109 Calories	337 mg Sodium	3 g Protein
2 g Total Fats	21 g Carbohydrates	
1 mg Cholesterol	5 g Dietary Fiber	

INGREDIENTS

- 1 sliced Celery Stalk
- 1 sliced Carrot
- ½ chopped red Bell Pepper
- ½ sliced Zucchini
- 2 minced cloves Garlic
- ½ tbsp. Chili Powder
- 7 oz. diced Tomatoes (unsalted)
- 1 cup Water
- ½ tsp. Kosher Salt
- 4 tbsp. non-fat Sour Cream
- Chopped Cilantro
- ¼ cup dry Bulgur, cooked

DIRECTIONS

- Sauté all the vegetables except tomatoes in the oil on "high" heat of slow cooker.
- Cook on "high" for 10 mins.
- Add the chili powder. Cook for 30 secs.
- Pour water, tomatoes and salt into the slow cooker.
- Cook on "low" for 1 hr.
- Now, add in the bulgur.
- Mix them well.
- Serve it in soup bowls along with the sour cream and cilantro.

21. Mac n Cheese Cauliflower

Cooking Time: 2 hrs 5 mins
Servings: About 4

Nutrition Facts (Estimated Amount Per Serving)

234 Calories	88 mg Sodium	13 g Protein
10 g Total Fats	23 g Carbohydrates	
30 mg Cholesterol	2 g Dietary Fiber	

INGREDIENTS

- ½ chopped Cauliflower head
- 1 cup of Milk (1%)
- ½ tsp. Mustard Powder
- ½ cup Swiss Cheese, shredded
- 1/8 cup Bread Crumbs (Japanese style – whole wheat)
- Canola Oil
- ¾ cup Elbow Macaroni
- ½ tbsp. Corn Starch
- ½ cup low-sodium Cheddar Cheese
- 1/8 tsp. ground Black Pepper

DIRECTIONS

- Cook the cauliflower in slow cooker for 20 mins. Remove the cauliflower and add the macaroni.
- Cook macaroni until soft.
- In a pan, pour milk, mustard powder and cornstarch.
- When the texture becomes thick, add in the pepper and cheese.
- Now, coat the slow cooker with oil. Pour in the milk sauce.
- Put the macaroni and cauliflower in the slow cooker.
- Cook on "low" for 1 hr.
- Cook continuously for next 20 mins, but uncovered.
- Add the chicken into the slow cooker. Combine cornstarch, soy sauce, sherry vinegar and broth along with pepper.
- Place the steaks in 1 tsp hot oil in slow cooker for 2 mins.
- Cook again on "low" for 1 hr.
- Leave it for 5 mins untouched before serving

22. French Style Onion Dip

Cooking Time: 30 mins
Servings: About 4

Nutrition Facts (Estimated Amount Per Serving)
151 Calories
2 g Total Fats
140 mg Sodium
28 mg Cholesterol
9 g Carbohydrates
5 g Dietary Fiber
5 g Protein

INGREDIENTS
- 1 tbsp. Olive Oil
- 1 minced clove Garlic
- ½ cup of low-fat Greek-style Yogurt
- 1/16 tsp. Kosher Salt
- ½ chopped White Onion
- ½ cup low-fat Sour Cream
- 1 tbsp. low-sodium Worcestershire Sauce
- 1/16 tsp. cracked Black Pepper

DIRECTIONS
- Heat oil in the slow cooker. Sauté the garlic and onion.
- Add the rest of the ingredients.
- Cook on low for 30 mins.
- Garnish with chives (minced). Serve with vegetables.

Delicious Poultry & Seafood

23. Turkey, Potatoes & Green Beans

Cooking Time: 4 hrs 30 mins
Servings: About 4

Nutrition Facts (Estimated Amount Per Serving)
138.9 g Calories
1.5 g Total Fat
9.2 mg Cholesterol
138.3 mg Sodium
26.9 g Carbohydrates
2.3 g Dietary Fiber
4.6 g Protein

INGREDIENTS
- Green Beans (large can)
- 4 Potatoes
- 1 pkg, Smoked Turkey Sausage

DIRECTIONS
- Place beans in the slow cooker.
- Slice the sausages and potatoes and add them to the beans.
- Pour water to cover the ingredients in the cooker.
- Stir and cook for 4 hrs.

24. Chicken and Rice

Cooking Time: 4 hrs 20 mins
Servings: About 6

Nutrition Facts (Estimated Amount Per Serving)
128.7 Calories
1.2 g Total Fat
43.5 mg Cholesterol
208.5 mg Sodium
9.5 mg Carbohydrates
0.8 g Dietary Fiber
19.3 g Protein

INGREDIENTS
- ½ lb fresh Mushroom
- ½ cup chopped Onion
- 1 lb diced Chicken
- 1 tsp. Chicken bouillon
- 1 tsp. Poultry Seasoning
- ¼ tsp. Salt
- 2 cups Water
- ¾ cup uncooked Rice

DIRECTIONS
- Slice the mushrooms.
- Grease the skillet with the oil.
- Sauté the chicken, mushrooms and onion for 15 mins.
- Add the seasoning and sautéed chicken to the slow cooker.
- Cook the chicken for 3-4 hrs. on low.
- When chicken is partially cooked, add the rice.
- Cook till the rice is done.
- Serve hot.

Cooking Time: 7 hrs 20 mins
Servings: About 8

Nutrition Facts (Estimated Amount Per Serving)

308 Calories

14 g Total Fat

118 mg Cholesterol

327 mg Sodium

3 mg Carbohydrates

0 g Dietary Fiber

38 g Protein

INGREDIENTS

- 3 lbs. Turkey Breast (halved and boneless)
- 2 tbsp. melted Butter
- 2 tbsp. Parsley (dried)
- ½ tbsp. Tarragon (dried)
- ½ tsp. Salt
- 1/8 tsp. Pepper
- 4 ½ ounces Mushrooms, sliced
- ½ cup Chicken Broth or White Wine
- 2 tbsp. Corn Starch

DIRECTIONS

- Place turkey in the slow cooker. Coat the turkey with the butter.
- Sprinkle the spices on the turkey.
- Place mushrooms on top of the turkey.
- Pour wine or broth over the turkey.
- Cook on "low" for 7 hrs.
- Transfer the turkey to a platter.
- Now, mix cornstarch with ¼ cup of water.
- Add the starch mixture to the slow cooker. Stir well.
- Boil for 2 mins.
- Serve turkey with the gravy.

26. Chicken and Lemon-filled Tacos

Cooking Time: 6 hrs 10 mins
Servings: 6

Nutrition Facts (Estimated Amount Per Serving)

291 Calories	674 mg Sodium	28 g Protein
3 g Total Fat	37 mg Carbohydrates	
63 mg Cholesterol	2 g Dietary Fiber	

INGREDIENTS

- 1 ½ pounds Chicken Breasts (halved and boneless)
- 3 tbsp. Lime Juice
- Lemon Zest
- 1 tbsp. Chili Powder
- 1 cup Corn (frozen)
- 12 Tortillas (wheat)
- 1 cup chunky Salsa
- Sour Cream
- Mexican Cheese
- Shredded Lettuce
- Jalapeo

DIRECTIONS

- Place chicken in slow cooker
- Pour lime juice and chili powder on the chicken
- Cook on "low" for 6 hrs.
- Transfer the chicken to a platter.
- Now, shred the chicken.
- Place the chicken into the slow cooker again.
- Add in the corn along with the salsa.
- Cook for 30 more mins.
- Fill tortillas with chicken and remaining ingredients.
- Serve warm.

27. Chicken and Green Beans

Cooking Time: 4 hrs
Servings: 5

Nutrition Facts (Estimated Amount Per Serving)
278 Calories
10 g Total Fat
134 mg Cholesterol
270 mg Sodium
8 mg Carbohydrates
0 g Dietary Fiber
32 g Protein

INGREDIENTS

- 2 lbs. Chicken Breasts
- ½ lbs. trimmed Green Beans
- 1 ¼ lbs. diced Potatoes
- ¼ cup Olive Oil
- 1/3 cup Lemon Juice
- 1 tsp. Oregano (dried)
- 1 tsp. Cilantro (dried)
- ¼ tsp. Pepper
- ¼ tsp. Onion Powder
- 2 minced cloves Garlic

DIRECTIONS

- Place chicken in the slow cooker.
- Arrange beans along the sides of the chicken.
- Next, repeat the process with potatoes.
- In a bowl, mix all the remaining ingredients.
- Pour the mixture over the arranged chicken, beans and potatoes.
- Cook on "high" for 4 hrs.
- Serve.

28. Barbecue Roasted Chicken

Cooking Time: 6 hrs 20 mins
Servings: About: 8
Nutrition Facts (Estimated Amount Per Serving)

239 Calories   397 mg Sodium   39 g Protein
5 g Total Fat   17 mg Carbohydrates
64 mg Cholesterol   1 g Dietary Fiber

INGREDIENTS
- 5 lbs. Roasting Chicken
- 1 tbsp. Garlic Powder
- ½ tsp. Kosher Salt
- ¼ cup Brown Sugar (light)
- 1 tbsp. Onion Powder
- 1 tbsp. Thyme (dried)
- 1 tbsp. Paprika
- 2 tsp. Cayenne Pepper
- 1 tsp. Black Pepper (ground)
- 1 tsp. Lemon Zest
- 1 tsp. Cumin (ground)
- Juice of 1 Lemon
- ½ cup Water

DIRECTIONS
- Rinse and pat dry the chicken.
- Mix all the ingredients except lemon juice in a bowl.
- Coat this mixture evenly on chicken.
- Place chicken on the slow cooker rack.
- Season the chicken with lemon.
- Cook on "low" for 6 hrs.
- Transfer the chicken to the cutting board when done.
- Discard the bones and skin and slice.
- Serve the chicken on heated plates.

29. Belgian Endive Chicken

Cooking Time: 6 hrs
Servings: About 8

Nutrition Facts (Estimated Amount Per Serving)

262 Calories	146 mg Sodium	2 g Protein
25 g Total Fat	4 mg Carbohydrates	
97 mg Cholesterol	2 g Dietary Fiber	

INGREDIENTS

- 2 pounds Chicken Thighs (skinless and boneless)
- 2 tbsp. Caraway Seeds
- ¼ tsp. Kosher Salt
- Ground Black Pepper
- 3 diced heads Belgian Endive
- 1 minced Bacon Strip
- 2 sliced tart apples
- ½ cup unsweetened Apple Juice

DIRECTIONS

- Rinse and pat dry the chicken.
- Season the chicken with pepper ,caraway seeds and salt.
- Roll up the thighs.
- Place them on the bottom of the slow cooker.
- Now, arrange a layer of endive in the slow cooker.
- Spread the Bacon strip evenly on the endive.
- Add a layer of Apple slices.
- Add apple juice to the slow cooker.
- Cook on "low" for 6 hrs.
- Serve the chicken on heated plates.

30. Hunter Chicken

Cooking Time: 4 hrs 30 mins
Servings: About 6

Nutrition Facts (Estimated Amount Per Serving)

177 Calories	377 mg Sodium	19 g Protein
5 g Total Fat	18 mg Carbohydrates	
39 mg Cholesterol	3 g Dietary Fiber	

INGREDIENTS

- 2 cubed Potatoes
- 2 sliced Carrots
- 6 ounces sliced Mushrooms
- 2 pounds Chicken Breasts (skinless and boneless)
- 2 tsp. o Olive Oil
- 1 sliced Onion
- 5 minced cloves Garlic
- 2 sliced Red Bell Peppers
- ½ cup Tomato Paste
- ½ cup Dry White Wine
- 1 tsp. Thyme (dried)
- 1 tsp. Rosemary (dried)
- 1 tsp. ground Black Pepper

DIRECTIONS

- Place carrots, mushrooms and potatoes on the bottom of the slow cooker.
- Add chicken.
- Season with pepper, rosemary and thyme.
- In a separate pan,sauté onion and garlic in oil for 3 mins.
- Add in the bell peppers and sauté again for 3 mins.
- Add tomato paste and cook for 2 mins.
- Now, add wine and pour the mixture into the slow cooker.
- Cook on "low" for 4 hrs.
- Serve in heated bowls.

31. Artichoke Chicken

Cooking Time: 6 hrs 10 mins
Servings: About 6

Nutrition Facts (Estimated Amount Per Serving)

160 Calories   457 mg Sodium   15 g Protein
8 g Total Fat   10 mg Carbohydrates
35 mg Cholesterol   3 g Dietary Fiber

INGREDIENTS

- 1 tsp. Paprika
- 1 tsp. Cayenne Pepper
- 2 pounds Chicken Pieces (skinless and boneless)
- 2 tbsp. Olive Oil
- 3 tbsp. Balsamic Vinegar (white)
- 2 minced cloves of Garlic
- 2 sliced leeks (green and white)
- 8 ounces Artichoke Hearts
- 1 cup Chicken Broth or White Wine

DIRECTIONS

- Season the chicken with Cayenne and paprika.
- Sauté chicken pieces for 2 mins in oil.
- Transfer the chicken to the slow cooker.
- In same pan, cook leeks, vinegar and garlic for 1 min.
- Add the artichokes along with broth or wine.
- Transfer them to slow cooker.
- Cook on "low" for 6 hrs.
- Serve the chicken on heated plates.

32. Peppered Cod

Cooking Time: 2 hrs 5 mins
Servings: About 4

Nutrition Facts (Estimated Amount Per Serving)
201 Calories
6 g Total Fat
101 mg Cholesterol
121 mg Sodium
1 mg Carbohydrates
1 g Dietary Fiber
39 g Protein

INGREDIENTS
- 1 ½ pounds Cod filets
- 1 tsp. Lemon Zest
- 2 tsp. Olive Oil
- 2 tbsp. Balsamic Vinegar
- ½ tsp. cracked Black Pepper

DIRECTIONS
- Divide a foil paper into one big portion and 4 small packets.
- Coat the foil and fish with the oil. Use pepper, lemon zest and vinegar to coat the fish.
- Wrap the fish with the foil tightly.
- Cook on "high" for 2 hrs.
- Serve hot.

33. Turkey Gumbo

Cooking Time: 5 hrs 30 mins
Servings: About 6

Nutrition Facts (Estimated Amount Per Serving)

155 Calories	313 mg Sodium	22 g Protein
8 g Total Fat	16 mg Carbohydrates	
207 mg Cholesterol	5 g Dietary Fiber	

INGREDIENTS

- ½ cup minced Turkey Ham
- 2 sliced stalks Celery
- 2 tsp. Olive Oil
- 1 sliced Onion
- 1 chopped Green Bell Pepper
- 2 minced cloves Garlic
- 14 ounces diced Tomatoes
- 2 cups o Chicken Broth
- 1 tsp. Worcestershire Sauce
- 1 pound cleaned Shrimp
- ¼ tsp. Kosher Salt
- 10 ounces thawed frozen Okra
- 1 tsp. Thyme (dried)
- 1 pound Crabmeat (frozen)

DIRECTIONS

- Sauté the ham in the oil.
- Transfer it to slow cooker.
- In the same pan, sauté garlic, pepper, onion and celery for 10 mins.
- Transfer them to slow cooker too.
- Now, pour Worcestershire sauce, salt, broth, thyme and tomatoes into the slow cooker.
- Cook on "low" for 4 hrs.
- When done, add crabmeat, okra and shrimp to the cooker and cook again on "high" for 20 more mins.
- Serve hot in heated bowls.

34. Salmon and Sweet Potato Chowder

Cooking Time: 4 hrs
Servings: About 4

Nutrition Facts (Estimated Amount Per Serving)

391 Calories	320 mg Sodium	37 g Protein
27 g Total Fat	39 mg Carbohydrates	
94 mg Cholesterol	7 g Dietary Fiber	

INGREDIENTS

- 1 tbsp. Butter
- 1 minced clove o Garlic
- 1 chopped Onion
- 2 tsp. Dill Weed
- 3 tbsp. o all-purpose Flour
- Ground Black Pepper
- 2 cups Milk
- 2 cups Sweet Potatoes (diced)
- 2 cups Chicken Broth
- 1 ½ cups Corn Kernels
- 1 tsp. Lemon Zest
- 12 ounces sliced Salmon Fillets
- 3 tbsp. Lemon Juice

DIRECTIONS

- Sauté pepper, dill, garlic and onion in butter in a pan.
- Add in the flour and cook for 2 mins.
- Pour broth and then milk to the pan. Simmer.
- Pour the mixture to the slow cooker and add the sweet potatoes.
- Cook on "low" for 4 hrs.
- Add in the salmon and cook again on "low" for 20 more mins.
- Now, stir in the lemon zest, lemon juice along with the pepper.
- Serve hot in heated bowls.

35. Chicken in Italian Sauce

Cooking Time: 4 hrs 20 mins
Servings: 2

Nutrition Facts (Estimated Amount Per Serving)

281 Calories	10 g Carbohydrates
8 g Total Fats	3 g Dietary Fiber
109 mg Cholesterol	38 g Protein
733 mg Sodium	

INGREDIENTS

- 6 oz. Chicken Breast (skinless and boneless)
- Olive Oil
- ¼ tsp. Kosher Salt
- ¼ sliced green Bell Pepper
- 1/8 tsp. ground Black Pepper
- 1 minced clove Garlic
- ½ chopped yellow Onion
- ½ tsp. Italian Seasoning
- 7.5 oz. diced Tomatoes (unsalted)
- 1/8 cup Red wine

DIRECTIONS

- Coat the chicken with pepper and salt.
- Sauté chicken in oil for 6 mins. Transfer the chicken to a plate.
- In slow cooker, pour ½ tbsp. olive oil and heat on "high."
- Sauté bell pepper, garlic and onion for 5 mins.
- Add the tomatoes.
- Cook on "low" for 2 hrs.
- Cook continuously for next 20 mins but uncovered.
- Add the chicken into the slow cooker.
- Cook again on "low" for 2 hrs.
- Serve immediately.

36. Sesame Salmon Fillets

Cooking Time: 30 mins
Servings: About 4

Nutrition Facts (Estimated Amount Per Serving)

319 Calories
21 g Total Fats
81 mg Cholesterol
204 mg Sodium
31 g Carbohydrates
1 g Dietary Fiber
31 g Protein

INGREDIENTS

- 2 tbsp. Sesame Oil
- ¼ tsp. Sea Salt
- ¼ tsp. Black Pepper (cracked)
- 1 tbsp. Vinegar
- 4 tsp. Sesame Seeds (black)
- ¼ tsp. Ginger (ground)
- 4 skinless Salmon fillets

DIRECTIONS

- Coat the slow cooker with oil. Set the cooker on "high".
- Place the salmon in the cooker. Drizzle the sesame seeds, pepper, salt and ginger on the salmon.
- Turn after 3 mins and repeat the procedure.
- Add vinegar and cook on "high" for 20 mins.
- Transfer the salmon to a plate. Serve immediately

Beef and Pork

37. Pork Roast

Cooking Time: 10 hrs
Servings: About 8

Nutrition Facts (Estimated Amount Per Serving)
162.8 Calories
3.5 g Total Fat
83.3 mg Cholesterol
919.9 mg Sodium
6.1 mg Carbohydrates
0.5 g Dietary Fiber
28.8 g Protein

INGREDIENTS
- 2 lbs Pork Roast (Sirloin)
- 1 envelope Lipton Onion Soup Mix
- 1 can Chicken Soup
- 1 tsp. Thyme (dried)
- 1 tsp. Rosemary (dried)
- ¼ tsp. Red Pepper Flakes
- ½ tsp. ground Black Pepper
- 2 cups Water

DIRECTIONS
- Mix all the ingredients in the slow cooker.
- Cook on "low" for 10 hrs.
- Serve hot

38. Barbeque Beef

Cooking Time: 9 hrs
Servings: About 12

Nutrition Facts (Estimated Amount Per Serving)
265.7 Calories
4.9 g Total Fat
81.6 mg Cholesterol
106.8 mg Sodium
23.9 mg Carbohydrates
0 g Dietary Fiber
29.0 g Protein

INGREDIENTS
- 3 lbs Chuck Roast (boneless)
- 1 tsp. Garlic Powder
- Salt
- 1 tsp. Onion Powder
- Pepper to taste
- 18 ounces Barbeque Sauce

DIRECTIONS
- After placing roast in the cooker, sprinkle on the seasoning.
- Now, pour barbeque sauce over the roast.
- Cook the roast on "low" for 8 hrs.
- Transfer the roast to plate and shred.
- Now, add the shredded roast back in the cooker and cook for one more hour.
- Serve hot

39. Savory Pork

Cooking Time: 9 hrs
Servings: About 2

Nutrition Facts (Estimated Amount Per Serving)

425 Calories	819.4 mg Sodium	4.7 g Dietary Fiber
18.7 g Total Fat	33.2 mg Carbohydrates	24.6 g Protein
66.7 mg Cholesterol		

INGREDIENTS

- ½ tbsp. Extra-Virgin Olive Oil
- 1 small sliced Onion
- 8 small Potatoes
- ½ tsp. ground Black Pepper
- Pinch of Salt
- ½ tsp. Garlic Powder
- 1 tbsp. fresh Sage (rubbed)
- 1 tbsp. fresh Rosemary (crushed)
- 1 tsp. Thyme (ground)
- 2 trimmed Loin Pork Chops
- 15-ounces low-fat Mushroom Soup
- ¼ cup White Wine

DIRECTIONS

- Place oil, potatoes and onion in the slow cooker. Sprinkle on seasoning.
- Toss well to coat.
- Remove fat from Pork chops.
- Place them over the vegetables in slow cooker.
- In a bowl, mix wine and mushroom soup well.
- Pour the mixture over the chops.
- Cook on "low" heat for 6 hrs.
- Serve hot.

40. Smoked Sausage and Cabbage

Cooking Time: 10 hrs
Servings: 4-6
Nutrition Facts (Estimated Amount Per Serving)
244.4 Calories
10.5 g Total Fat
75 mg Cholesterol
945.5 mg Sodium
18.3 mg Carbohydrates
3.8 g Dietary Fiber
15.5 g Protein
INGREDIENTS
- 1 small head Cabbage, shredded
- 1 large chopped Onion
- 1 ½ pounds Smoked Turkey Sausage
- 7 small Red Potatoes
- 1 cup Apple Juice
- 1 tbsp. Dijon Mustard
- 1 tbs. Cider Vinegar
- 2 tbsp. Brown Sugar
- 1 tsp. Caraway Seeds
- Pepper to taste
DIRECTIONS
- In a 6 qt. cooker, place onion, cabbage & sausage in a layer.
- Cook on high for 10 mins
- In a bowl, whisk rest of the ingredients.
- Now, pour this mixture on the cabbage.
- Sprinkle on the seasonings.
- Cook on "low" for 10 hrs.
- Serve hot.

41. Roast Beef

Cooking Time: 5 hrs
Servings: About 5

Nutrition Facts (Estimated Amount Per Serving)
293 Calories
8.2 g Total Fat
136.1 mg Cholesterol
372 mg Sodium
2.9 mg Carbohydrates
0.3 g Dietary Fiber
48.6 g Protein

INGREDIENTS
- 2.5 lbs Chuck Roast
- 1 tbsp. Worcestershire Sauce
- 1 tbsp. Soy Sauce
- 2 tbsp. Balsamic Vinegar
- 1 chopped Onion

DIRECTIONS
- In a slow cooker, pour all the ingredients over the roast.
- Cook on "low" for 5 hrs.
- Serve hot.

42. Pork and Pineapple Roast

Cooking Time: 7 hrs
Servings: About 4

Nutrition Facts (Estimated Amount Per Serving)
465.1 Calories
10.7 g Total Fat
134.3 mg Cholesterol
107.2 mg Sodium
44.3 mg Carbohydrates
3 g Dietary Fiber
47.49 g Protein

INGREDIENTS
- 2 pounds Pork Roast
- 1.5 tsp. Salt
- ½ tsp. Black Pepper
- 20-ounces Pineapple Chunks
- 1 cup Cranberries (chopped)

DIRECTIONS
- Season the roast on all sides.
- Place all the ingredients in the slow cooker.
- Cook on "low" for 7 hrs.
- Serve hot.

43. Beef with Carrots and Turnips

Cooking Time: 8 hrs
Servings: About 12

Nutrition Facts (Estimated Amount Per Serving)

318 Calories

11 g Total Fat

99 mg Cholesterol

538 mg Sodium

13 mg Carbohydrates

3 g Dietary Fiber

35 g Protein

INGREDIENTS

- 1 tbsp. Kosher Salt
- 2 tsp. Cinnamon (ground)
- ½ tsp. Allspice (ground)
- ½ tsp. Pepper (ground)
- ¼ tsp. Cloves (ground)
- 3 ½ pounds Chuck Roast
- 2 tbsp. Olive Oil (extra virgin)
- 1 chopped Onion
- 3 sliced cloves Garlic
- 1 cup Red Wine
- 28 ounces whole Tomato
- 5 sliced carrots
- 2 diced Turnips
- Chopped Basil

DIRECTIONS

- Mix all dry spices in a bowl. Season the beef with the spice mixture.
- In a skillet, brown the beef for 5 mins in oil.
- Remove it and place it into the slow cooker.
- In same pan, sauté onion and garlic.
- Add the wine and tomatoes.
- Boil the wine mixture.
- Transfer the wine mixture to the slow cooker.
- Cook them on "low" for 8 hrs.
- Serve it hot after slicing the beef.

44. Pot Roast in a Slow Cooker

Cooking Time: 6 hrs
Servings: About 6

Nutrition Facts (Estimated Amount Per Serving)

382 Calories	395 mg Sodium	51 g Protein
11 g Total Fat	8 mg Carbohydrates	
141 mg Cholesterol	1 g Dietary Fiber	

INGREDIENTS

- 1 chopped large, sweet Onion
- 1 cup sliced Portobello Mushrooms
- 3 lb. Beef Chuck Roast
- ½ tsp. Salt
- ¼ tsp. Pepper
- 1 cup Beef Broth or Red Wine
- 1 tbsp. Brown Sugar
- 1 tbsp. Dijon Mustard
- 1 tsp. Worcestershire Sauce
- 2 tbsp. Corn Starch

DIRECTIONS

- Place mushrooms and onions in the slow cooker.
- Coat roast with pepper and salt.
- Place the roast into the slow cooker.
- In a bowl, mix all the ingredients except cornstarch.
- Pour the mixture into the slow cooker.
- Cook on "low" for 6 hrs.
- In a bowl, mix cornstarch with 2 tbsp. of water. Stir well.
- Add the mixture to the slow cooker.
- Cook again for 30 mins.
- Slice beef and serve on heated plates.

45. Pepper Steak

Cooking Time: 9 hrs
Servings: About 6
Nutrition Facts (Estimated Amount Per Serving)
349 Calories
23 g Total Fat
107 mg Cholesterol
371 mg Sodium
11 mg Carbohydrates
2 g Dietary Fiber
36 g Protein

INGREDIENTS

- 1 ½ pounds boneless Beef Steaks
- 2 diced Onions
- 1 chopped clove Garlic
- ½ tsp. chopped Ginger
- ½ cup Beef Broth
- 3 tbsp. Tamari Sauce
- ¼ cup Cold Water
- 2 green and 2 red (sliced) bell peppers
- 2 sliced Tomatoes

DIRECTIONS

- Cut the beef into 6 equal pieces.
- In a bowl, combine ginger, tamari sauce and garlic. Marinate the beef for 2 hrs. at least.
- In the slow cooker, spread pepper and onion on the bottom.
- Place beef along with the marinade in the slow cooker.
- Pour broth into the slow cooker.
- Cook on "low" for 8 hrs.
- Serve the beef on heated plates

46. Beef Brisket

Cooking Time: 8 hrs
Servings: About 12

Nutrition Facts (Estimated Amount Per Serving)

283 Calories

15 g Total Fat

128 mg Cholesterol

385 mg Sodium

7 mg Carbohydrates

2 g Dietary Fiber

44 g Protein

INGREDIENTS

- 5 pounds Beef Brisket (trimmed)
- 2 minced cloves Garlic
- ½ tsp. Black Pepper
- 2 tbsp. Brown Sugar
- 2 tsp. Paprika (smoked)
- 2 sliced Onions
- 1 ½ cup Beef Broth
- 3 diced Carrots
- 3 sliced Parsnips
- 14 ounces diced Tomatoes

DIRECTIONS

- In a bowl, mix paprika, brown sugar, black pepper and garlic.
- Coat beef with paprika mixture and place it into the slow cooker.
- Now, place all the remaining ingredients in layers.
- Cook on "low" for 8 hrs.
- Transfer the beef to a cutting board.
- Leave it for 10 mins at least.
- Slice and serve with the cooked vegetables.

47. Pork with Squash and Apples

Cooking Time: 6 hrs 15 mins
Servings: About 4

Nutrition Facts (Estimated Amount Per Serving)

322 Calories   350 mg Sodium   19 g Protein
25 g Total Fat   10 mg Carbohydrates
74 mg Cholesterol   3 g Dietary Fiber

INGREDIENTS

- 4 boneless Pork Chops
- Ground Black Pepper
- 1 sliced Onion
- 2 tsp. Olive Oil
- 1 minced clove Garlic
- 1 sliced Red Bell Pepper
- ½ tsp. ground Cumin
- ½ tsp. ground Cinnamon
- ½ cup Chicken Broth
- ½ cup Coconut Milk
- 1 diced tart Apple
- 1 cup cubed Squash
- 2 tbsp. chopped Parsley

DIRECTIONS

- Sauté the pork chops in oil for 6 mins.
- Transfer them to slow cooker.
- In same pan, , sauté rest of the ingredients except apple, broth, squash and coconut milk.
- Pour the mixture into the slow cooker.
- Now, add the rest of the ingredients.
- Cook on "low" for 6 hrs.
- Serve the Pork chops on heated plates after garnishing with parsley.

48. Lemony Pork Roast

Cooking Time: 8 hrs 15 mins
Servings: About 8

Nutrition Facts (Estimated Amount Per Serving)

317 Calories	174 mg Sodium	49 g Protein
15 g Total Fat	12 mg Carbohydrates	
106 mg Cholesterol	5 g Dietary Fiber	

INGREDIENTS

- 4 boneless Pork Chops
- Ground Black Pepper
- 1 sliced Onion
- 2 tsp. Olive Oil
- 1 minced clove Garlic
- 1 sliced Red Bell Pepper
- ½ tsp. ground Cumin
- ½ tsp. ground Cinnamon
- ½ cup Chicken Broth
- ½ cup Coconut Milk
- 1 diced tart Apple
- 1 cup cubed Squash
- 2 tbsp. chopped Parsley

DIRECTIONS

- Place all ingredients except Pork Chops in the slow cooker.
- Put the pork chops in afterwards.
- Cook on "low" for 8 hrs.
- When cooked, transfer the pork to a cutting board.
- Leave it for 10 mins and then slice.
- Transfer the pork and vegetables to heated plates and serve.

49. Chili Verde

Cooking Time: 8 hrs 10 mins
Servings: About 6
Nutrition Facts (Estimated Amount Per Serving)
452 Calories
27 g Total Fat
202 mg Cholesterol
269 mg Sodium
25 mg Carbohydrates
5 g Dietary Fiber
50 g Protein

INGREDIENTS

- 2-3 pounds Pork shoulder
- 1 cup Beef Broth
- 2 cups Yellow Potatoes (cubed)
- 2 sliced Poblano Chiles
- 3 sliced Green Chiles
- 1 cup Tomatillos (chopped)
- 4 minced cloves Garlic
- 1 diced Onion
- ½ tsp. Cumin(ground)
- ¼ tsp. Black Pepper (ground)
- 6 steamed corn Tortillas

DIRECTIONS

- In a pan, sauté the pork chops in oil for 6 mins.
- Place all the ingredients except tortillas in slow cooker.
- Add pork chops.
- Cook on "low" for 8 hrs.
- Serve the Chili Verde with tortillas on heated plates.

50. Pork Chops and White Beans

Cooking Time: 4 hrs
Servings: 2
Nutrition Facts (Estimated Amount Per Serving)

458 Calories

21 g Total Fats

78 mg Cholesterol

357 mg Sodium

34 mg Carbohydrates

8 g Dietary Fiber

33 g Protein

INGREDIENTS

- 1 ½ tsp. Olive Oil
- ¼ tsp. Black Pepper
- ½ diced Carrot
- ¼ cup Chicken Broth (low sodium)
- ¼ tsp. Rosemary (dried)

- ¼ tsp. Kosher Salt
- 2 pork chops (boneless)
- ½ diced Yellow Onion
- 1 minced clove Garlic
- 7.5 oz. Cannellini Beans
- Chopped Parsley

DIRECTIONS

- Season the chops with pepper and salt.
- Sauté them in oil for 3 min on each side.
- Transfer them to a plate.
- In same pan, sauté rest of the ingredients except Parsley.
- Cook for 4 mins.
- Transfer the cooked mixture to the slow cooker along with the broth.
- Cook on "low" for 2 hrs.
- Add the tomatoes along with the herbs and beans.
- Cook for 1 more hour on low.
- Place the pork into the slow cooker.
- Cook for 10 mins on "high".
- Serve after garnishing with parsley.

Soups & Stews

51. Chicken and Rice Stew

Cooking Time: 8 hrs
Servings: About 6
Nutrition Facts (Estimated Amount Per Serving)
245.5 Calories
6.2 g Total Fat
35.1 Cholesterol
1761.1 mg Sodium
21.2 Carbohydrates
1.5 g Dietary Fiber
25.2 g Protein
INGREDIENTS
- 2 med. Carrots
- 2 med. Leeks
- 1 cup Rice (uncooked)
- 12 oz Boneless Chicken (without skin)
- 1 tsp. Thyme
- ½ tsp. Rosemary
- 3 cans Chicken Broth (14 oz. each)
- 1 can cream of Mushroom Soup (10.75 oz.)
- ½ cup Onion (chopped)
- 1 clove Garlic

DIRECTIONS
- Place all the ingredients in a slow cooker.
- Cover the slow cooker.
- Cook on low for 7 or 8 hrs. or on high for 4 hrs.
- Serve hot.

52. Chicken and Tortilla soup

Cooking Time: 6 -8 hrs
Servings: About 12

Nutrition Facts (Estimated Amount Per Serving)

93.4 Calories	11.9 g Carbohydrates
1.9 g Total Fat	2.1 g Dietary Fiber
18.6 Cholesterol	8.3 g Protein
841.3 mg Sodium	

INGREDIENTS

- 3 Chicken Breasts (boneless and skinless)
- 15 ounces diced Tomatoes
- 10 ounces Enchilada Sauce
- 1 chopped Onion (med.)
- 4 ounces chopped Chili Pepper (green)
- 3 minced cloves Garlic
- 2 cups Water
- 14.5-ounces Chicken Broth (fat free)
- 1 tbsp. Cumin
- 1 tbs. Chile Powder
- 1 tsp. Salt
- ¼ tsp. Black Pepper
- Bay Leaf
- 1 tbsp. Cilantro (chopped)
- 10 ounces Frozen Corn
- 3 tortillas, cut into thin slices

DIRECTIONS

- Place all the ingredients in the slow cooker.
- Stir well to mix.
- Cook on low heat for 8 hrs. or on high heat for 6 hrs.
- Transfer the chicken breasts to a plate and shred.
- Add chicken to other ingredients.
- Serve hot, garnished with tortilla slices.

53. Stuffed Pepper Soup

Cooking Time: 8 hrs 10 mins
Servings: 6

Nutrition Facts (Estimated Amount Per Serving)
216.1 Calories
5.1 g Total Fat
43.4 mg Cholesterol
480.7 mg Sodium
21.8 mg Carbohydrates
2.5 g Dietary Fiber
18.8 g Protein

INGREDIENTS
- 1 lb ground Beef (drained)
- 1 chopped Onion (large)
- 2 cups Tomatoes (diced)
- 2 chopped Green Peppers
- 2 cups Tomato Sauce
- 1 tbs. Beef Bouillon
- 3 cups Water
- Pepper
- 1 tsp. of Salt
- 1 cup of cooked Rice (white)

DIRECTIONS
- Place all ingredients in a cooker.
- Cook for 8 hrs. on "low".
- Serve hot.

54. Ham and Pea Soup

Cooking Time: 8 hrs
Servings: About 8

Nutrition Facts (Estimated Amount Per Serving)
118.6 Calories
1.9 g Total Fat
15.9 mg Cholesterol
828.2 mg Sodium
14.5 mg Carbohydrates
5.1 g Dietary Fiber
11.1 g Protein

INGREDIENTS
- 1 lb. Split Peas (dried)
- 1 cup sliced Celery
- 1 cup sliced Carrots
- 1 cup sliced Onion
- 2 cups chopped Ham (cooked)
- 8 cups Water

DIRECTIONS
- Place all the ingredients in the slow cooker.
- Cook on "high" for 4 hrs.
- Serve hot.

55. Vegetable Stew

Cooking Time: 8 hrs
Servings: 4-6

Nutrition Facts (Estimated Amount Per Serving)
186 Calories
1.2 g Total Fat
0 mg Cholesterol
692.9 mg Sodium
38.8 mg Carbohydrates
10.3 g Dietary Fiber
8.3 g Protein

INGREDIENTS
- 1 cup Corn
- 1 cup Hominy
- 1 cup Green Beans
- 1 can Peas (black eyed)
- 1 cup Lima Beans
- 1 cup chopped Carrots
- 1 cup chopped Celery
- 1 cup Onion
- 1 can Tomato Sauce (small)
- 2 cups Vegetable Broth
- 2 tbsp. Worcestershire Sauce

DIRECTIONS
- Place all the ingredients in the slow cooker.
- Cook on "low" for 8 hrs.
- Serve hot.

56. Pea Soup

Cooking Time: 8 hrs
Servings: About 8

Nutrition Facts (Estimated Amount Per Serving)
122.7 Calories
2 g Total Fat
24 mg Cholesterol
780.6 mg Sodium
15 mg Carbohydrates
5.2 g Dietary Fiber
11.8 g Protein

INGREDIENTS
- 16 oz. Split Peas (dried)
- 1 cup chopped Baby Carrots
- 1chopped Onion (white)
- 3 Bay Leaves
- 10 oz. cubed Turkey Ham
- 4 cubes Chicken Bouillon
- 7 cups Water

DIRECTIONS
- Rinse and drain peas.
- Place all the ingredients in the slow cooker.
- Cook on "low" for 8 hrs. Serve hot.

57. Soup for the day

Cooking Time: 10 hrs 10 mins
Servings: About 8

Nutrition Facts (Estimated Amount Per Serving)

259.6 Calories
6.7 g Total Fat
29.8 mg Cholesterol
699.2 mg Sodium
31.6 mg Carbohydrates
4.6 g Dietary Fiber
18.9 g Protein

INGREDIENTS

- 1 Beef Steak (cubed)
- 1 chopped Onion (med.)
- 1 tbsp. Olive Oil
- 5 thinly sliced med. Carrots
- 4 cups Cabbage
- 4 diced Red Potatoes
- 2 diced Celery Stalks
- 2 cans Tomatoes, diced
- 2 cans Beef Broth
- 1 tsp. Sugar
- 1 can Tomato Soup
- 1 tsp. Parsley Flakes (dried)
- 2 tsp. Italian Seasoning

DIRECTIONS

- In a skillet, sauté onion and steak in oil.
- Transfer the sautéed mixture to the slow cooker.
- Add rest of the ingredients to the slow cooker.
- Cook on "low" for 10 hrs.
- Serve hot.

58. Chicken and Sweet Potato Stew

Cooking Time: 5 hrs
Servings: About 5

Nutrition Facts (Estimated Amount Per Serving)300 Calories
6 g Total Fat
50 mg Cholesterol
520 mg Sodium
38 mg Carbohydrates
5 g Dietary Fiber
18 g Protein

INGREDIENTS

- 6 Chicken Thighs
- 2 pounds peeled and sliced Sweet Potatoes
- ½ pound sliced Mushrooms
- 6 Shallots (halved)
- 4 peeled cloves Garlic
- 1 cup White Wine (dry)
- 2 tsp.chopped Rosemary
- 1 tsp. Salt
- ½ tsp Pepper (ground)
- ½ tbsp. Vinegar (white wine)

DIRECTIONS

- Place all the ingredients in the slow cooker.
- Cook on "low" for 5 hrs.
- Serve hot after removing bones.

59. Pork and Fennel Stew

Cooking Time: 8 hrs 10 mins
Servings: About 5

Nutrition Facts (Estimated Amount Per Serving)

249 Calories	303 mg Sodium	20 g Protein
13 g Total Fat	9 mg Carbohydrates	
70 mg Cholesterol	3 g Dietary Fiber	

INGREDIENTS

- 8 cups of Fennel (thinly sliced)
- 1 Onion (halved and sliced)
- 2 ½ pounds Pork Shoulder, cubed
- 1 ½ tsp. Kosher Salt
- 1 ½ tsp. Pepper (grounded)
- 2 tbsp. Olive Oil (extra virgin)
- ¾ cup White Wine (dry)
- 4 cloves minced Garlic
- 1 tbsp. chopped Rosemary
- 2 tsp. chopped Oregano
- 28 ounce can Tomatoes (whole)

DIRECTIONS

- Place onion and fennel on the bottom of the slow cooker.
- In another dish, sprinkle the pepper and salt on pork.
- In a skillet, pour in oil.
- Brown the pork that will fit in the skillet for 5 mins.
- Transfer the pork to the slow cooker.
- Repeat the process for rest of the pork.
- Add wine to pan and scrape the brown pieces in the pan.
- Add the rest of the ingredients to the slow cooker.
- Cook on "low" for 8 hrs.
- Serve hot.

60. Vegetable Garbanzo Stew

Cooking Time: 6 hrs 10 mins
Servings: About 2

Nutrition Facts (Estimated Amount Per Serving)

287 Calories	258 mg Sodium	13 g Protein
8 g Total Fat	41 mg Carbohydrates	
0 mg Cholesterol	9 g Dietary Fiber	

INGREDIENTS

- 3 cups diced Butternut Squash
- 3 peeled and diced Carrots
- 2 chopped Onions
- 3 minced cloves o Garlic
- 4 cups Vegetable Stock (low sodium)
- 1 cup Red Lentils
- 2 tbsp. Tomato Paste (unsalted)
- 2 tbsp. minced Ginger
- 2 tsp. Cumin (ground)
- 1 tsp. Turmeric
- ¼ tsp. Saffron
- 1 tsp. Pepper (ground)
- ¼ cup Lemon Juice
- 16 ounces Garbanzo Beans
- ½ cup chopped Peanuts (unsalted)
- ½ cup chopped Cilantro

DIRECTIONS

- Sweat the vegetables in a Dutch Oven.
- Brown the Onion.
- Pour in the stock and scrape any pieces of vegetables sticking to the pan.
- Now, add all the ingredients to the slow cooker.
- Cook on "low" for 6 hrs.
- Stir the lemon juice into the slow cooker before serving.
- Garnish with peanuts and serve.

61. Catalan Stew

Cooking Time: 8 hrs 30 mins
Servings: About 6

Nutrition Facts (Estimated Amount Per Serving)

421 Calories   439 mg Sodium   55 g Protein
26 g Total Fat   16 mg Carbohydrates
5 mg Cholesterol   3 g Dietary Fiber

INGREDIENTS

- 2 chopped slices Pancetta
- 2 tbsp. Olive Oil (extra virgin)
- 3 pounds Chuck Roast
- 1 cup Red Wine (dry)
- 2 chopped Onions
- 3 cups Beef Broth (low sodium)
- 2 tbsp. Tomato Paste
- 4 minced cloves Garlic
- 2 crushed Cinnamon Sticks
- 4 sprigs Thyme
- 3 slices of peeled Orange
- 1 ounce chopped Dark Chocolate
- 3 tbsp. chopped Parsley

DIRECTIONS

- Sauté pancetta in oil till crisp.
- Transfer it to the slow cooker.
- Using the same pan, sauté beef.
- Transfer beef to the slow cooker as well.
- Now, sauté onion for 3 mins.
- Add wine, tomato paste and vinegar to the sauté pan and stir to mix.
- Transfer this wine mixture to the slow cooker and sprinkle on the rest of the ingredients except parsley.
- Cook on "low" for 8 hrs. Stir when done.
- Add the chocolate and cook on "high" for 10 mins.
- Remove cinnamon, orange peel and thyme.
- Serve after garnishing with parsley.

62. Pork Stew Caribbean Style

Cooking Time: 7 hrs 30 mins
Servings: About 4

Nutrition Facts (Estimated Amount Per Serving)

452 Calories	269 mg Sodium	50 g Protein
27 g Total Fat	25 mg Carbohydrates	
202 mg Cholesterol	5 g Dietary Fiber	

INGREDIENTS

- 1 ½ pounds cubed Pork Loin
- 1 tbsp. Thyme (dried)
- ¼ tsp. Allspice (ground)
- White Pepper (ground)
- 1 pound Yukon Potatoes, quartered
- 3 diced Carrots
- 1-inch piece of Ginger Root, chopped
- 2 tsp. Worcestershire Sauce
- 1 chopped clove Garlic
- ½ cup sliced Scallions
- 1 cup diced Tomatoes

DIRECTIONS

- Coat the pork with pepper, allspice and thyme.
- Place remaining ingredients except scallions in the slow cooker.
- Put in the pork along with the Worcestershire sauce.
- Place the tomatoes on top.
- Cook on "low" for 7 hrs.
- Serve the stew with scallions.

63. Fish Stew

Cooking Time: 4 hrs 10 mins
Servings: About 6
Nutrition Facts (Estimated Amount Per Serving)

207 Calories	536 mg Sodium	32 g Protein
4 g Total Fat	5 mg Carbohydrates	
168 mg Cholesterol	1 g Dietary Fiber	

INGREDIENTS

- 1 sliced Leek
- 2 tsp. Olive Oil (extra virgin)
- 1 sliced Onion
- 4 minced cloves of Garlic
- ½ cup of White Wine (dry)
- 4 Bay Leaves
- ¼ cup Water
- ½ tsp. Black Pepper (cracked)
- 1 piece Orange Peel
- 2 tbsp. chopped Parsley
- 1 ½ pounds o Haddock Fillets
- 12 ounces peeled Shrimp

DIRECTIONS

- Arrange garlic, leek and onion on the bottom of slow cooker.
- Add i water and wine.
- Put in the peppercorn, orange peel and bay leaves.
- Cook on "high" for 2 hrs.
- Now, add shrimp and fish.
- Cook again on "high" for 2 hrs.
- Remove the orange peel and bay leaves.
- Garnish with parsley and olive oil.
- Serve hot in heated bowls.

64. Tuna and Red Pepper Stew

Cooking Time: 4 hrs 15 mins
Servings: About 6

Nutrition Facts (Estimated Amount Per Serving)
107 Calories
3 g Total Fat
8 mg Cholesterol
200 mg Sodium
15 mg Carbohydrates
2 g Dietary Fiber
5 g Protein

INGREDIENTS
- 1 tbsp. Olive Oil
- 1 chopped Onion
- 1 minced clove Garlic
- ½ cup White Wine (dry)
- ¼ tsp. Pepper Flakes (red)
- 14 ounce diced Tomatoes
- 1 tsp. Paprika
- 1 pound scrubbed red potatoes
- 2 sliced roasted Bell Peppers (red)
- 2 pounds f Tuna Fillet
- 3 tbsp. Cilantro (chopped)

DIRECTIONS
- Except for paprika, tuna and peppers, place all the ingredients in the slow cooker and cook on "high" for 2 hrs.
- Add paprika, tuna, and peppers.
- Cook again on "high" for 2 hrs.
- Garnish with cilantro.
- Serve hot.

65. Chipotle Squash Soup

Cooking Time: 4 hrs 20 mins
Servings: About 6

Nutrition Facts (Estimated Amount Per Serving)
102 Calories
11 g Total Fat
2 mg Cholesterol
142 mg Sodium
22 mg Carbohydrates
3 g Dietary Fiber
4 g Protein

INGREDIENTS
- 6 cups Butternut Squash (cubed)
- ½ cup chopped Onion
- 2 tsp. Adobo Chipotle
- 2 cups Chicken Broth
- 1 tbsp. Brown Sugar
- ¼ cup Tart Apple (chopped)
- 1 cup Yogurt (Greek style)
- 2 tbsp. Chives (chopped)

DIRECTIONS
- Except yogurt, chives and apple, place all the ingredients in the slow cooker.
- Cook on "low" for 4 hrs.
- Now, in a blender or food processer, puree the cooked ingredients.
- Transfer puree to slow cooker.
- Add the yogurt and cook on "Low" for 20 more mins.
- Garnish with chives and apples.
- Serve hot in heated bowls.

66. Kale Verde

Cooking Time: 6 hrs
Servings: 6
Nutrition Facts (Estimated Amount Per Serving)
257 Calories
22 g Total Fat
3 mg Cholesterol
239 mg Sodium
27 mg Carbohydrates
6 g Dietary Fiber
14 g Protein
INGREDIENTS
- ¼ cup Olive Oil (extra virgin)
- 1 Yellow Onion (large)
- 2 cloves Garlic
- 2 ounces Tomatoes, dried
- 2 cups Yellow Potatoes (diced)
- 14 ounce Tomatoes (diced)
- 6 cups Chicken Broth
- White Pepper (ground)
- 1 pound o chopped Kale

DIRECTIONS
- Sauté onion for 5 mins in oil.
- Add the garlic and sauté again for 1 mins.
- Transfer the sautéed mixture to the slow cooker.
- Now, put the rest of the ingredients except pepper into the slow cooker.
- Cook on "low" for 6 hrs.
- Season with white pepper to taste.
- Serve hot in heated bowls

67. Escarole with Bean Soup

Cooking Time: 6 hrs
Servings: About 6
Nutrition Facts (Estimated Amount Per Serving)

98 Calories	115 mg Sodium	8 g Protein
33 g Total Fat	14 mg Carbohydrates	
1 mg Cholesterol	3 g Dietary Fiber	

INGREDIENTS

- 1 tbsp. Olive Oil
- 8 crushed cloves Garlic
- 1 cup chopped Onions
- 1 diced Carrot
- 3 tsp. Basil (dried)
- 3 tsp. Oregano (dried)
- 4 cups Chicken Broth
- 3 cups chopped Escarole
- 1 cup o Northern Beans (dried)
- Parmesan Cheese (grated)
- 14 ounces o Tomatoes (diced)

DIRECTIONS

- Sauté garlic for 2 mins in oil using a large soup pot.
- Except for the cheese, broth and beans, add the rest of the ingredients and cook for 5 mins.
- Transfer the cooked ingredients to the slow cooker.
- Mix in the broth and beans.
- Cook on "low" for 6 hrs.
- Garnish with cheese.
- Serve hot in heated bowls

68. Chicken Squash Soup

Cooking Time: 5 hrs 30 mins
Servings: 3

Nutrition Facts (Estimated Amount Per Serving)

158 Calories	699 mg Sodium	3 g Protein
6 g Total Fats	24 mg Carbohydrates	
0 mg Cholesterol	6 g Dietary Fiber	

INGREDIENTS

- ½ Butternut Squash (large)
- 1 clove Garlic
- 1 ¼ qrts. broth (vegetable or chicken)
- 1/8 tsp. Pepper (white)
- ½ tbsp. chopped Parsley
- 2 minced Sage leaves
- 1 tbsp. Olive Oil
- ¼ chopped Onion (white)
- 1/16 tsp. Black Pepper (cracked)
- 1/2 tbsp. of Pepper Flakes (chili)
- ½ tsp. chopped Rosemary

DIRECTIONS

- Preheat oven to 400 degrees.
- Grease a baking sheet.
- Roast the squash cut side down in preheated oven for 30 mins.
- Transfer it to a plate and let it cool.
- Sauté onion and garlic in the oil.
- Now, scoop out the flesh from the roasted squash and add to the sautéed onion & garlic.
- Mash all of them well.
- Now, pour ½ qrt of the broth in the slow cooker. Add the squash mixture. Cook on "low" for 4 hrs.
- Using a blender, make a smooth puree.
- Transfer the puree to the slow cooker.
- Add in the rest of the broth and other ingredients.
- Cook again for 1 hr. on "high".
- Serve in heated soup bowls.

69. Veggie and Beef Soup

Cooking Time: 4 hrs
Servings: About 4

Nutrition Facts (Estimated Amount Per Serving)

217 Calories	728 mg Sodium	22 g Protein
7 g Total Fats	17 mg Carbohydrates	
53 mg Cholesterol	5 g Dietary Fiber	

INGREDIENTS

- 1 chopped Carrot
- 1 chopped Celery Rib
- ¾ l. Sirloin (ground)
- 1 cup Water
- ½ Butternut Squash (large)
- 1 clove Garlic
- ½ qrt Beef broth
- 7 ounces diced Tomatoes (unsalted)
- ½ tsp. Kosher Salt
- 1 tbsp. chopped Parsley
- ¼ tsp. Thyme (dried)
- ¼ tsp. Black Pepper (ground)
- ½ Bay Leaf

DIRECTIONS

- Sauté all the vegetables in oil.
- Push the vegetables to the side and place sirloin in the center. Sauté, using a spoon to crumble the meat.
- When cooked, combine with the vegetables on the sides of the pan.
- Now, pour rest of the ingredients in the slow cooker.
- Add in cooked meat and vegetables.
- Stir well.
- Cook on "low" for 3 hrs.
- Serve in soup bowls.

70. Collard, Sweet Potato and Pea Soup

Cooking Time: 4 hrs
Servings: About 4

Nutrition Facts (Estimated Amount Per Serving)
172 Calories
4 g Total Fats
11 mg Cholesterol
547 mg Sodium
24 mg Carbohydrates
4 g Dietary Fiber
11 g Protein

INGREDIENTS
- 3.5 oz. Ham Steak, chopped
- ½ chopped Yellow Onion
- ½ lb. sliced Sweet Potatoes
- ¼ tsp. Red Pepper (hot and crushed)
- ½ cup frozen Peas (black eyed)
- ½ tbsp. Canola Oil
- 1 minced clove of Garlic
- 1 ½ cup Water
- ¼ tsp. Salt
- 2 cups Collard Greens (julienned and without stems)

DIRECTIONS
- Sauté ham with garlic and onion in oil.
- In slow cooker, place other ingredients except collard greens and peas.
- Add in the ham mixture.
- Cook on "low" for 3 hrs.
- Now, add collard green and peas and cook again for an hour on "low".
- Serve in soup bowls.

71. Bean Soup

Cooking Time: 5 hrs
Servings: 4
Nutrition Facts (Estimated Amount Per Serving)
258 Calories
19 g Total Fats
2 mg Cholesterol
620 mg Sodium
25 mg Carbohydrates
11 g Dietary Fiber
8 g Protein
INGREDIENTS

- ½ cup Pinto Beans (dried)
- ½ Bay Leaf
- 1 clove Garlic
- ½ Onion (white)
- 2 cups Water
- 2 tbsp. Cilantro (chopped)
- 1 cubed Avocado
- 1/8 cup White Onion (chopped)
- ¼ cup Roma Tomatoes (chopped)
- 2 tbsp. Pepper Sauce (chipotle)
- ¼ tsp. Kosher Salt
- 2 tbsp. chopped Cilantro
- 2 tbsp. Low Fat Monterrey Jack Cheese, shredded

DIRECTIONS

- Place water, salt, onion, pepper, garlic, bay leaf and beans in the slow cooker.
- Cook on high for 5-6 hours.
- Discard the Bay leaf.
- Serve in heated bowls.

72. Brown Rice and Chicken Soup

Cooking Time: 4 hrs
Servings: About 4

Nutrition Facts (Estimated Amount Per Serving)

208 Calories	540 mg Sodium	20 g Protein
6 g Total Fats	18 mg Carbohydrates	
71 mg Cholesterol	2 g Dietary Fiber	

INGREDIENTS

- 1/3 cups Brown Rice
- 1 chopped Leek
- 1 sliced Celery Rib
- 1 ½ cups water
- ½ tsp. Kosher Salt
- ½ Bay Leaf
- 1/8 tsp. Thyme (dried)
- ¼ tsp. Black Pepper (ground)
- 1 tbsp. chopped Parsley
- ½ qrt Chicken Broth (low sodium)
- 1 sliced Carrot
- ¾ lb. of Chicken Thighs (skin and boneless)

DIRECTIONS

- In a saucepan, boil 1 cup of water with ½ tsp. of Salt.
- Add the rice.
- Cook for 30 mins on medium flame.
- Brown chicken pieces in the oil.
- Transfer the chicken to a plate when done.
- In same pan, sauté the vegetables for 3 mins.
- Now, place the chicken pieces in the slow cooker. Add water and broth.
- Cook on "low" for 3 hrs.
- Now, add the rest of the ingredients, the rice last.
- Cook again for 10 mins on "high".
- After discarding Bay leaf, serve in soup bowls

73. Broccoli Soup

Cooking Time: 3 hrs
Servings: About 2

Nutrition Facts (Estimated Amount Per Serving)

291 Calories   227 mg Sodium   17 g Protein
14 g Total Fats   28 mg Carbohydrates
24 mg Cholesterol   6 g Dietary Fiber

INGREDIENTS

- 4 cups chopped Broccoli
- ½ cup chopped Onion (white)
- 1 ½ cup Chicken Broth (low sodium)
- 1/8 tsp. Black Pepper (cracked)
- 1 tbsp. Olive Oil
- 1 Garlic Clove
- 1/16 tsp. Pepper Flakes (chili)
- ¼ cup Milk (low fat)

DIRECTIONS

- In the slow cooker, cover the broccoli with water and cook for an hour on "high."
- Set aside after draining.
- Sauté onion and garlic in oil and transfer them to slow cooker when done.
- Add the broth.
- Cook on "low" for 2 hrs.
- Transfer the mixture to a blender and make a smooth puree. Add black pepper, milk and pepper flakes to the puree.
- Boil briefly.
- Serve the soup in heated bowls.

Drinks & Salads

74. Papaya and Greens Drink

Cooking Time: 1 hr 15 mins
Servings: About 1

Nutrition Facts (Estimated Amount Per Serving)
114 Calories
2 g Total Fats
0 mg Cholesterol
32 mg Sodium
25 mg Carbohydrates
7 g Dietary Fiber
3 g Protein

INGREDIENTS
- ½ cup Spinach
- 1/3 cup Water
- ½ chopped Green Apple
- ½ tbsp. Flaxseeds
- ½ cup Kale (chopped)
- ¼ cup chopped Cucumber (unpeeled)
- ½ cup o chopped Papaya

DIRECTIONS
- In a blender, place all the ingredients and make a smooth puree.
- Pour the puree into the slow cooker.
- Cook on "low" for 1 hr.
- Serve in a glass or a mug.

75. Papaya and Coconut Drink

Cooking Time: 1 hr 20 mins
Servings: About 1

Nutrition Facts (Estimated Amount Per Serving)
158 Calories
3 g Total Fats
7 mg Cholesterol
39 mg Sodium
26 mg Carbohydrates
2 g Dietary Fiber
8 g Protein

INGREDIENTS
- ½ diced Papaya (peeled and seeded)
- 1 tbsp. Wheat Germ
- ½ cup Yogurt (Low Fat)
- ¼ tsp. sweetener (non-caloric)
- ½ cup Coconut Water

DIRECTIONS
- In a blender, place all the ingredients and make a smooth puree.
- Pour the puree into the slow cooker.
- Cook on "low" for 1 hr.
- Serve in a glass or a mug.

76. Kale and Apple Drink

Cooking Time: 1 hrs 15 mins
Servings: About 2

Nutrition Facts (Estimated Amount Per Serving)
171 Calories
10 g Total Fats
0 mg Cholesterol
31 mg Sodium
19 mg Carbohydrates
5 g Dietary Fiber
5 g Protein

INGREDIENTS
- 1 chopped Sweet Apple
- 4 tbsp. Sunflower Seeds
- 2 cups drained Kale (stemmed)
- 2/3 cups Vinegar (apple cider)
- 12 Ice Cubes
- 16 Mint Leaves

DIRECTIONS
- In a blender, place all the ingredients and make a smooth puree.
- Pour the puree into the slow cooker.
- Cook on "low" for 1 hr.
- Serve in a glass or a mug.

77. Shrimp, Bean and Mango Salad

Cooking Time: 4 hrs 20 mins
Servings: About 2

Nutrition Facts (Estimated Amount Per Serving)
213 Calories
2 g Total Fats
107 mg Cholesterol
679 mg Sodium
36 g Carbohydrates
7 g Dietary Fiber
18 g Protein

INGREDIENTS
- 1/8 cup Water
- 1 peeled and diced Mango
- 7.5 oz. Black Beans (drained)
- 1 tbsp. chopped Mint or Cilantro
- 1/3 lb. Shrimp (peeled)
- 1 tbsp. Lime Juice
- ¼ minced Jalapeño
- 1 tbsp. minced Onion (red)

DIRECTIONS
- Place shrimp and cover with water in the slow cooker.
- Cook on "low" for 4 hrs. Let cool.
- Place rest of the ingredients in the salad bowl. Add shrimp.
- Toss thoroughly. Serve.

78. Olive and Mushroom Salad

Cooking Time: 4 hrs 20 mins
Servings: About 2

Nutrition Facts (Estimated Amount Per Serving)
44 Calories
4 g Total Fats
35 mg Cholesterol
199 mg Sodium
6 g Carbohydrates
1 g Dietary Fiber
0.7 g Protein

INGREDIENTS
- 1 tbsp. Vegan Margarine
- ¼ cup sliced Mushrooms(shiitake)
- ¼ cup chopped mushrooms of Hen of woods
- ¼ cup Oyster Mushrooms (sliced)
- 1/8 cup sliced Kalamata Olives
- ¼ tsp. Black Pepper (cracked)
- 1/8 tsp. o Kosher Salt
- 6 leaves o Romaine Lettuce
- 2 sliced Roma Tomatoes

DIRECTIONS
- Place all the ingredients in the slow cooker.
- Cook on "low" for 2 hrs. Remove from cooker and allow to cool.
- Arrange Roma tomatoes and lettuce leaves in a plate. Drizzle with freshly prepared dressing and serve.

79. Spinach and Strawberry Salad

Cooking Time: 2 hrs 15 mins
Servings: About 2
Nutrition Facts (Estimated Amount Per Serving)
211 Calories
16 g Total Fats
0 mg Cholesterol
85 mg Sodium
14 g Carbohydrates
5 g Dietary Fiber
4 g Protein
INGREDIENTS
- 1 tbsp. Olive Oil (extra virgin)
- ½ lb. hulled Strawberries
- 1 tbsp. Water
- 1 tbsp. Vinegar (balsamic)
- 3 oz. Baby Spinach
- 1 tsp. o Poppy Seeds
- ½ cup o Goat Cheese (crumbled)
- ¼ cup chopped Hazelnuts
- Black Pepper (ground)

DIRECTIONS
- Puree half the Strawberries in a blender.
- Slice the remainder.
- Mix oil, vinegar and water into the freshly prepared Puree.
- Cook on "low" for 1 hr.
- Now, add in the pepper, salt and poppy seeds.
- In a bowl, toss all the ingredients.
- Garnish with goat cheese, strawberries and hazelnut.
- Serve.

Side Dishes

80. Quinoa Curry

Cooking Time: 4 hrs
Servings: 8

Nutrition Facts (Estimated Amount Per Serving)

297 Calories   364 mg Sodium   28 g Protein
18 g Total Fat   9 mg Carbohydrates
167 mg Cholesterol   1 g Dietary Fiber

INGREDIENTS

- 1 chopped Sweet Potato
- 2 cups Green Beans
- ½ diced Onion (white)
- 1 diced Carrot
- 15 oz Chick Peas (organic and drained)
- 28 oz. Tomatoes (diced)
- 29 oz Coconut Milk
- 2 minced cloves of Garlic
- ¼ cup Quinoa
- 1 tbs. Turmeric (ground)
- 1 tbsp. Ginger (grated)
- 1 ½ cups Water
- 1 tsp. of Chili Flakes
- 2 tsp. of Tamari Sauce

DIRECTIONS

- Place all the ingredients in the slow cooker.
- Add 1 cup of water.
- Stir well.
- Cook on "high" for 4 hrs.
- Serve with rice

81. Lemon and Cilantro Rice

Cooking Time: 6 hrs
Servings: About 4

Nutrition Facts (Estimated Amount Per Serving)
56 Calories
0.3 g Total Fats
174 mg Sodium
12 g Carbohydrates
1 g Dietary Fiber
1 g Protein

INGREDIENTS
- 3 cups Vegetable Broth (low sodium)
- 1 ½ cups Brown Rice (uncooked)
- Juice of2 lemons
- 2 tbsp. chopped Cilantro

DIRECTIONS
- In a slow cooker, place broth and rice.
- Cook on "low" for 5 hrs.
- Check the rice for doneness with a fork.
- Add the lemon juice and cilantro before serving.

82. Chili Beans

Cooking Time: 4 hrs
Servings: About 5

Nutrition Facts (Estimated Amount Per Serving)
343 Calories
11 g Total Fat
123 mg Cholesterol
308 mg Sodium
9 mg Carbohydrates
3 g Dietary Fiber
29 g Protein

INGREDIENTS
- 1 ½ cup chopped Bell Pepper
- 1 ½ cup sliced Mushrooms (white)
- 1 cup chopped Onion
- 1 tbsp. Olive Oil
- 1 tbsp. Chili Powder
- 2 chopped cloves Garlic
- 1 tsp. chopped Chipotle Chili
- ½ tsp. Cumin
- 15.5 oz drained Black Beans
- 1 cup diced Tomatoes (no salt)
- 2 tbsp. chopped Cilantro

DIRECTIONS
- Place all the ingredients in the slow cooker.
- Cook on "high" for 4 hrs. Serve

83. Bean Spread

Cooking Time: 4 hrs
Servings: About 20

Nutrition Facts (Estimated Amount Per Serving)
298 Calories
18 g Total Fat
10 mg Cholesterol
298 mg Sodium
30 mg Carbohydrates
3 g Dietary Fiber
19 g Protein

INGREDIENTS

- 30 ounces Cannellini Beans
- ½ cup Broth (chicken or veg)
- 1 tbsp. Olive Oil
- 3 minced cloves Garlic
- ½ tsp. Marjoram
- ½ tsp. Rosemary
- 1/8 tsp. Pepper
- Pita Chips
- 1 tblsp. Olive Oil

DIRECTIONS

- Place olive oil, beans, broth, marjoram, garlic, rosemary and pepper in the slow cooker.
- Cook on "low" for 4 hrs.
- Mash the mixture and transfer to a bowl.
- Serve with Pita.

84. Stir Fried Steak, Shiitake and Asparagus

Cooking Time: 2 hrs 10 mins
Servings: 3

Nutrition Facts (Estimated Amount Per Serving)

182 Calories   157 mg Sodium   20 g Protein
7 g Total Fats   10 mg Carbohydrates
45 mg Cholesterol   3 g Dietary Fiber

INGREDIENTS

- 1 tbsp. Sherry (dry)
- 1 tbsp. Vinegar (rice)
- ½ tbsp. Soy Sauce (low sodium)
- ½ tbsp. Cornstarch
- 2 tsp. Canola Oil
- ¼ tsp. Black Pepper (ground)
- 1 minced clove Garlic
- ½ lb. sliced Sirloin Steak
- 3 oz. Shiitake Mushrooms
- ½ tbsp. minced Ginger
- 6 oz. sliced Asparagus
- 3 oz. Peas (sugar snap)
- 2 sliced scallions
- ¼ cup Water

DIRECTIONS

- Combine cornstarch, soy sauce, sherry vinegar, broth and pepper.
- Place the steaks in 1 tsp hot oil in slow cooker for 2 mins.
- Transfer the steaks to a plate.
- Sauté ginger & garlic in the remaining oil.
- Add in the mushrooms, peas and asparagus.
- Add water and cook on "low" for 1 hr.
- Add the scallions and cook again for 30 mins on low.
- Change the heat to "high" and add the vinegar.
- When the sauce has thickened, transfer the steaks to the slow cooker.
- Stir well and serve immediately.

85. Chickpeas and curried veggies

Cooking Time: 4 hrs
Servings: About 2

Nutrition Facts (Estimated Amount Per Serving)

271 Calories   207 mg Sodium   7 g Protein
11 g Total Fats   39 g Carbohydrates
2 mg Cholesterol   8 g Dietary Fiber

INGREDIENTS

- ½ tbsp. Canola Oil
- 2 sliced Celery Ribs
- 1/8 tsp. Cayenne Pepper
- ¼ cup Water
- 2 sliced Carrots
- 2 sliced red Potatoes (sliced)
- ½ tbsp. Curry Powder
- ½ cup o Coconut Milk (light)
- ¼ cup drained Chickpeas (low sodium)
- Chopped Cilantro
- ¼ cup Yogurt (low fat)

DIRECTIONS

- Sauté potatoes for 5 mins in oil.
- Add the carrots, celery and onion. Sauté for 5 more mins.
- Sprinkle on the curry powder and cayenne pepper. Stir well to combine.
- In slow cooker, pour water and coconut milk.
- Add in the potatoes.
- Cook on "low" for 3 hrs.
- Add chickpeas and cook for 30 more mins.
- Serve in bowls along with the yogurt and cilantro garnish.

86. Brussels Sprouts Casserole

Cooking Time: 4 hrs 15 mins
Servings: 3
Nutrition Facts (Estimated Amount Per Serving)
128 Calories
9 g Total Fats
56 mg Sodium
2 mg Cholesterol
5 g Carbohydrates
4 g Dietary Fiber
5 g Protein

INGREDIENTS

- ¾ lb. Brussels Sprouts
- 1 diced slice Pancetta
- 1 minced clove Garlic
- 1 tbsp. chopped Shallot
- ¼ cup pine nuts (toasted)
- ¼ tsp. Black Pepper (cracked)
- 4 tbsp. Water

DIRECTIONS

- Slice sprouts and place them in the slow cooker along with the water.
- Cook on "high" for 1 hr.
- Drain well.
- Remove the fat from Pancetta.
- Sauté the pancetta for 4 mins.
- Add the shallots, garlic and 1/8 cup of Pine Nuts to the sauté.
- Now, add the sprouts. Cook for 3 mins.
- Transfer the prepared mixture to the slow cooker. Add black pepper. 4 tbsp. of water and cook again on "low" for 2 hrs.
- Serve immediately.

87. Tasty Cauliflower

Cooking Time: 6 hrs 15 mins
Servings: 4

Nutrition Facts (Estimated Amount Per Serving)
150 Calories
14 g Total Fats
69 mg Sodium
6 g Carbohydrates
3 g Dietary Fiber
2.2 g Protein

INGREDIENTS
- 2 minced cloves Garlic
- 2 cups Cauliflower florets
- 2 tbsp. Olive Oil
- Pinch of Sea Salt
- ¼ tsp. Pepper Flakes (chili)
- Pinch of Black Pepper (cracked)
- 4 tbsp. Water
- Zest of ½ lemon

DIRECTIONS
- In a slow cooker, place cauliflower and oil.
- Add vinegar.
- Toss well to coat thoroughly.
- Put in the rest of the ingredients and toss again.
- Cook on "low" for 2 hrs. Serve immediately.

88. Artichoke and Spinach Dip

Cooking Time: 2 hrs 10 mins
Servings: About 2
Nutrition Facts (Estimated Amount Per Serving)
263 Calories
14 g Total Fats
537 mg Sodium
42 mg Cholesterol
18 g Carbohydrates
6 g Dietary Fiber
20 g Protein
INGREDIENTS

- 1/8 tsp. Basil (dried)
- 14 oz. chopped Artichoke Hearts
- 1 ½ cups Spinach
- ½ minced clove Garlic
- ¼ cup Sour Cream (low fat)
- ¼ cup shredded Cheese (Parmesan)
- ¼ cup Mozzarella Cheese (shredded)
- 1/8 tsp. Parsley (dried)
- ½ cup Yogurt (Greek)
- Pinch of Black Pepper
- Pinch of Kosher Salt

DIRECTIONS

- Boil spinach in water for 1 min.
- Drain the water. Set the spinach aside to cool and then chop.
- Puree all the ingredients including spinach in a blender.
- Transfer the mixture to the slow cooker.
- Add cheeses and cook for 1 hour on "low".
- Serve with sliced vegetables.

89. Apple Salsa

Cooking Time: 2 hrs
Servings: 3

Nutrition Facts (Estimated Amount Per Serving)
100 Calories
0.4 g Total Fats
50 mg Sodium
0 mg Cholesterol
20 g Carbohydrates
6 g Dietary Fiber
5 g Protein

INGREDIENTS

- 7 ½ oz. drained Black Beans
- ¼ cubed Apples (Granny Smith)
- ¼ chopped Chili Pepper (Serrano)
- 1/8 cup chopped Onion (red)
- 1 ½ tbsp. chopped Cilantro
- ¼ Lemon
- ¼ Orange
- Pinch of Sea Salt
- Pinch of Black Pepper (cracked)

DIRECTIONS

- Mix all the ingredients in the cooker (slow cooker).
- Cook on "low" for an hour.
- Transfer to a covered container and allow to cool for 1 hr.
- Serve.

Tasty Breakfasts and Desserts

90. Homemade Granola

Cooking Time: 55 mins
Servings: About 5

Nutrition Facts (Estimated Amount Per Serving)

205 Calories
5 mg Cholesterol
440 mg Sodium
41 mg Carbohydrates
3 g Dietary Fiber
7 g Protein

INGREDIENTS

- 1/8 cup Brown Sugar
- 1 tbsp. Water
- ½ tsp. Vanilla extract
- ½ tbsp. Vegetable Oil
- ½ cup Raisins
- ½ tsp. Cinnamon (ground)
- 2 cups Oats (rolled)
- ¼ cup Milk (low fat)
- ¼ cup Dates (chopped)

DIRECTIONS

- Except for raisins and dates, mix all the ingredients in a bowl. Make sure sugar is thoroughly dissolved.
- Grease the slow cooker and set it on "High". Cook the granola for 30 mins uncovered.
- Turn the slow cooker off.
- Add the raisins and dates and allow the granola to cool. Serve with milk

91. Apple with Oatmeal

Cooking Time: 10 hrs 15 mins
Servings: About 8

Nutrition Facts (Estimated Amount Per Serving)
264.5 Calories
7.1 g Total Fat
1.5 Cholesterol
28.7 mg Sodium
47.8 mg Carbohydrates
6.9 g Dietary Fiber
8.4 g Protein

INGREDIENTS
- 2 cups dry Oats (steel cut)
- 2 cups chopped Apples
- 1 cup of dried Cranberries (sweetened)
- 3 cup Water
- 1 cup Milk (low fat)
- 1 tbsp. ground Cinnamon
- 1 tsp. Pie Spice (pumpkin)
- 2 tsp. Margarine
- ½ cup o sliced Almonds
- ½ cup Pecans

DIRECTIONS
- Place margarine in the cooker.
- Except nuts, place all the ingredients into the cooker.
- On "warm" setting, cook for 10 hrs. Serve with nuts

92. Apple Crisp

Cooking Time: 4 hrs 10 mins
Servings: 5

Nutrition Facts (Estimated Amount Per Serving)
278 Calories
10 g Total Fat
134 mg Cholesterol
270 mg Sodium
8 mg Carbohydrates
0 g Dietary Fiber
32 g Protein

INGREDIENTS
- 1 cup Oatmeal
- 1 cup Brown Sugar
- 2 tbsp. Flour (all purpose)
- 1 tbsp. Sugar (granulated)
- 1 stick Butter
- 1 tsp. Cinnamon
- 1 lb. Apples (Granny Smith)

DIRECTIONS
- Peel and thinly slice the apples.
- Add flour and granulated sugar to the apples.
- Coat them well.
- Place them in the slow cooker.
- Now, add remaining ingredients except oats.
- Last, sprinkle the oatmeal on the apples.
- Cook on "high" for 4 hrs.
- Serve hot.

93. Pecan and Banana Cake

Cooking Time: 6 hrs 10 mins
Servings: About 3
Nutrition Facts (Estimated Amount Per Serving)
278 Calories
13 g Total Fats
34 mg Cholesterol
262 mg Sodium
34 mg Carbohydrates
4 g Dietary Fiber
9 g Protein

INGREDIENTS

- ½ cup Pastry Flour (wheat)
- ½ tbsp. Sugar
- ¼ cup unbleached Flour (all purpose)
- 1 tsp. Kosher Salt
- ¾ tsp. Baking Powder
- 1 egg white and 1 egg
- ¾ cup Milk (1%)
- ½ sliced Banana
- 1 tbsp. Canola Oil
- ¼ cup chopped Pecans

DIRECTIONS

- In a bowl, mix both flours, sugar, salt and baking powder.
- In another bowl, beat the egg white and egg with milk and 1 tbsp. of oil. Mash the banana and add to the eggs. Add pecans.
- Slowly, mix the egg mixture into the dry ingredients.
- Set parchment paper in the slow cooker.
- Now, pour the prepared banana batter in the slow cooker.
- Cook on "low" for 5 hrs.
- Turn the slow cooker off.
- Keep aside to let the cake stand for 10 mins.
- Serve.

94. Banana and Almond Spread

Cooking Time: 1 hrs 10 mins
Servings: 2

Nutrition Facts (Estimated Amount Per Serving)
338 Calories
13 g Total Fats
0 mg Cholesterol
153 mg Sodium
52 mg Carbohydrates
8 g Dietary Fiber
10 g Protein

INGREDIENTS
- 2 Bananas (large)
- 2 cups Almond Milk (unsweetened)
- 2 tbsp. Wheat Germ
- 2 tbsp. Almond Butter (unsalted)
- ¼ tsp. Cinnamon (ground)
- ¼ tsp. Vanilla Extract
- 6 Ice Cubes

DIRECTIONS
- Puree all the ingredients in a blender.
- Pour this puree in the slow cooker.
- Cook on "low" for 1 hr.
- Serve on Muffins or Bread.

95. Coconut Pudding

Cooking Time: 6 hrs 10 mins
Servings: About 4

Nutrition Facts (Estimated Amount Per Serving)
357 Calories
14 g Total Fats
137 mg Sodium
0 mg Cholesterol
52 g Carbohydrates
1.5 g Dietary Fiber
6 g Protein

INGREDIENTS

- 1/8 tsp. Salt
- ½ cup Rice (white)
- ½ quart Soy Milk
- ½ cup Sugar
- 1/16 cup Coconut (shredded)
- ¼ cup Margarine (Vegan)
- ½ tsp. Cinnamon

DIRECTIONS

- Place all ingredients in the slow cooker.
- Cook on "low" for 6 hrs. Serve.

96. Almond and Chocolate Bars

Cooking Time: 2 hrs
Servings: About 8
Nutrition Facts (Estimated Amount Per Serving)
303 Calories
20.5 g Total Fats
5.5 mg Sodium
0 mg Cholesterol
34 g Carbohydrates
4.5 g Dietary Fiber
4.5 g Protein

INGREDIENTS
- 14 oz. Chocolate Chips (semisweet)
- 2 cups Almonds (chopped)

DIRECTIONS
- Place all the ingredients in the slow cooker.
- Cook on "low" for 1 hr. Stir thoroughly every 15 mins.
- Arrange a sheet of wax paper.
- Spread the chocolate on the wax paper.
- Let the chocolate cool and slice it in the shape of bars.
- Serve.

97. Berry Yogurt

Cooking Time: 1 hr
Servings: About 3
Nutrition Facts (Estimated Amount Per Serving)
163 Calories
4 g Total Fats
47 mg Sodium
5 mg Cholesterol
20 g Carbohydrates
5 g Dietary Fiber
14 g Protein

INGREDIENTS
- ¾ cup Blueberries
- ¾ cup Strawberries (chopped)
- ¾ cup Raspberries
- ¾ tsp. Lemon Zest (grated)
- ¾ tsp. Orange Zest (grated)
- ¾ tbsp. Balsamic Vinegar
- Juice ¼ Orange
- 1 ½ cup Greek Yogurt (low fat)
- ¼ tsp. Vanilla Extract
- 3 tbsp. sliced Almonds (toasted)
- Black Pepper (cracked)

DIRECTIONS
- Place all the ingredients except yogurt and almonds in the slow cooker.
- Cook on "low" for 1 hr.
- Mash the berries.
- Divide the yogurt in bowls.
- Garnish with berry sauce and almonds.
- Serve.

98. Hot Fondue

Cooking Time: 1 hr
Servings: 8
Nutrition Facts (Estimated Amount Per Serving)
318 Calories
25 g Total Fats
16 mg Sodium
0 mg Cholesterol
26 g Carbohydrates
1.5 g Dietary Fiber
1.5 g Protein
INGREDIENTS
- ¼ Corn Syrup (light)
- ½ cup Soy Milk
- ½ cup Margarine (vegan)
- ½ tbsp. Vanilla Extract
- 8 oz. Chocolate Chips (semisweet and dark)
- Salt
DIRECTIONS
- Place all the ingredients except Vanilla and chocolate chips in the slow cooker.
- Cook on "low" for 1 hr.
- Stir once and again cook for another hr on "low". Add in rest of the ingredients. Mix well so that chocolate will melt thoroughly.
- Serve with fruit.

99. Crunchy Pears

Cooking Time: 2 hrs 10 mins
Servings: About 3

Nutrition Facts (Estimated Amount Per Serving)
201 Calories
0 g Total Fats
7 mg Sodium
0 mg Cholesterol
38 g Carbohydrates
6 g Dietary Fiber
4 g Protein

INGREDIENTS
- 2 ½ cups chopped Pear
- ½ tbsp. Lemon Juice
- 1 tbsp. Maple Syrup
- ¼ tsp. Nutmeg (grated)
- 1 tsp. Cornstarch
- ½ cup Granola (homemade)
- Canola Oil

DIRECTIONS
- Coat the slow cooker with canola oil.
- Place all the ingredients in the cooker.
- Cook on "low" for 2 hrs.
- Sprinkle on the Granola and leave it for 10 mins.
- Serve hot.

100. Peanut Cake

Cooking Time: 2 hrs
Servings: About 4
Nutrition Facts (Estimated Amount Per Serving)
281 Calories
11 g Total Fats
214 mg Sodium
0 mg Cholesterol
30 g Carbohydrates
1.5 g Dietary Fiber
5.5 g Protein
INGREDIENTS
- ½ cup Flour (almond)
- ½ cup Brown Sugar
- ¼ tsp. Baking Soda
- 1/3 cup Water
- ½ tsp. Baking Powder
- ½ cup Peanut Butter (low sodium)
- ½ tsp. Vanilla Extract
DIRECTIONS
- Mix all the dry ingredients in a bowl.
- In another bowl, combine all the wet ingredients.
- Combine all ingredients gradually.
- Coat the slow cooker with oil.
- Pour the mixture in.
- Cook on "low" for 1 hr.
- Serve.

Conclusion

Here we come to the end of the book. I hope that this attempt of encouraging you to live a healthy lifestyle by incorporating the DASH Diet will help you improve your health and achieve your weight loss goals as well as motivate you to stay on the DASH Diet.

DASH meals cooked in slow cookers won't just save your precious time but will also reduce the hassle of being physically present in the kitchen. You come home from work or play to delicious and healthy meals. However, as suggested earlier, it is recommended to do the preparation for cooking in advance, preferably the previous night. Next morning all you have to do is dump the meals in a slow cooker, adjust the heat settings and that is it!

Each recipe listed in the book will help you achieve your health and fitness goals and provide most of the nutrients that the body needs to function. Your body won't be deprived of any micronutrient or macronutrient. The DASH Diet will also assist in striking the right balance between saturated and unsaturated fats. DASH isn't a temporary weight loss program, rather, it is a long-term healthy eating program that can provide guaranteed and sustained results.

Made in the USA
Middletown, DE
26 March 2021